THE LABYRINTH OF THE HEART
Changed Myths for Changing Lives

Daniel Cohen

Copyright © Daniel Cohen 2010.
Drawings © Z*qhygoem 2011, © Cathy Dagg, and © Wen Fyfe 2011.
Front cover design © Marjorie Sutler 2011.
All rights reserved.

Except as covered by the Creative Commons license below and the permission for oral storytelling, you may not reproduce or transmit this publication or material from this publication in any form or by any means, electronic or mechanical, without permission in writing from the author. Such requests can be directed to d dot e dot cohen at qmul dot ac dot uk

Daniel Cohen asserts his moral right to be identified as the author of this book.

The individual stories and their notes (except for *Taste and See*, which is by Daniel Cohen, but is copyright Equinox Publications) are licensed under the Creative Commons Attribution-NonCommercial-ShareAlike License. To view a copy of this license, visit http://creativecommons.org/licenses/by-nc-sa/3.0/; or send a letter to Creative Commons, 171 2nd Street, Suite 300, San Francisco, California, 94105, USA. The images are not licensed in this way, but are subject to normal copyright restrictions.

Stories like to be told. Therefore Daniel Cohen specifically states that oral retelling of these stories (except for *Taste and See*) to a live audience is permitted provided due credit is given to the author and the book, and that any such use is considered by him to be non-commercial even if the performers are paid.

Dedicated to all those in whom the Goddess has shown Herself to me. Most especially to the memory of Asphodel Long (1921 — 2005), companion and guide on the journey. Her life and her work are good enough reasons for the world to turn.

ISBN 978-0-9513851-2-8
Published by Wood and Water, 77 Parliament Hill London NW3 2TH
http://www.decohen.com

Daniel draws on ancient texts, myths, ballads and tales with an insightful new twist, wry and uniquely his own.

It's a lovely little book, some of it absolutely great. I especially like the midrash on Eve.

Robin Williamson (bard, storyteller, founder-member of the Incredible String Band.)

These retellings are brave, beautiful and original, combining a genuine appreciation of the original myths and legends with a rigorous new system of ethics. They are a fresh illustration of the eternal truth that good stories will live for ever, providing that they can still find good storytellers to adapt them.

Ronald Hutton (author of *The Triumph of the Moon*, *The Pagan Religions of the Ancient British Isles*, and many other books and articles.)

Cohen's stories teach us insights into gender roles, especially those involving heroism today. They are self-conscious as he recognizes that they want to be told through him, but they are never boringly didactic. Story itself shines forth as creatrix/creator — not of banalities, but richly of fantasies.

This author sees behind stories' seams through his critical eye and voice. His Theseus (or Perseus) is no muscle-bound gym-rat, but a male who returns to Ariadne, having confronted his brother deep inside the labyrinth, and celebrates her re-weaving the crucial thread "as a connection now between the ordinary world and the mysteries of the deep labyrinth."

These are long-polished re-viewing and re-insighting narratives of classical and late-European versions of magical shoes and trees and tricksters, biblical midrashim, Goddesses and Scottish salmon, characters such as Arawn and Pwyll. They make me wish I had children to tell them to (oh, yeah, a buddy's girls, they'll giggle with delight). Notes at the end explain starting points for these engaging narratives.

William G. Doty (author of *Myths: a Handbook*, *Myths of Masculinity*, and other writings on myth.)

Myths are the eternal shapeshifters who mirror reality; their glory is that they are not fixed in one place. This witty, insightful book inspires us to incubate myths in the rich ground of daily life and discover how they can still surprise us. It boldly percolates through the bedrock of memory into the most immediate realms of experience. Some myths will taste familiar to you, while others carry the fresh-baked crust of new bread for the journey of life. Taste them for yourself!

Caitlín Matthews (author of *Sophia, Goddess of Wisdom*, *King Arthur's Raid*, *Mabon and the Guardians of Celtic Britain* and many other books.)

Daniel Cohen's retellings of Greek and Celtic myths take my breath away and make my spine tingle, pointing the way to a transformation of the cultures of domination that have shaped our world, causing so much damage to all of us and the web of life."
Carol P. Christ (author of *Rebirth of the Goddess* and *She Who Changes*.)

They're remarkable in many ways. First, his fables about men and the Goddess illuminate women and men's relationships with each other. More, the writing *transforms* these relationships.
Francesca De Grandis (author of *Bardic Alchemy: Enchanted Tales about the Quest for God/dess and Self*.)

This small but mould-shattering volume left me stunned and breathless many times over. There is much power in these stories that will inspire both male and female readers without leaving either feeling in any way less important or vital to the truth and power within the myths.
Wildheart

I have to tell you, without sentimentality, just how much the book has come to mean to me. As a woman, I recognised the Theseus who thought he had killed the animal in him, and am thankful that it was a stage in his journey. I am profoundly glad to know of the Theseus who embraced his brother and visits him at the appropriate time. This alone is such a healing story that I have told it to people I meet, writers and psychotherapists and friends. On an academic level, your Theseus was exactly what I needed to side-step the false duality of gender stereotypes in mythic material.
Sandy Hutchinson-Nunns

CONTENTS

Preface	1
Surprising the Soul: the Secret of Stories (Introduction)	2
The Story of The Story (the beginning)	7
The Heart of the Labyrinth	9
Face of Wisdom, Face of Dread	13
Maiden and Monster	19
Circe's Bard	21
The Ferryman	25
The Biggest Dung-Heap in the World	29
Happy the Land that Needs No Heroes	31
The First Casualty of War	34
The Sleeping Beauty	36
What Women Most Desire	40
The Singer's Lost Love	46
Of Power, Good Counsel, and Wisdom	49
Esmeralda's Quest	52
The Interpreter: or an Introduction to Hermeneutics	56
New Shoes for New Weather	60
A Successful Experiment?	64
Taste and See: a Midrash on Genesis 3:6 and 3:12	68
The Man who Did Not Like Spiders	71
The Mathematician who Had Little Wisdom	76
The Ballad of Jack Green (for Alan Acacia, a wise April fool)	80
Three Worlds, Two Queens, One Prince	82
The Seer in the Hawthorn Tree	88
Pity the Poor Emigrant	92
Johnny Faa's Indictment	95
The Dancer and the Dance	99
The Story of The Story (completed)	102
Notes on the Myths	103
Booklist	126
Acknowledgements	132
Illustrations	134

PREFACE

I've read no better storyteller than Daniel Cohen. And my standards are high. So if my words seem like hype, be assured: I mean them from the bottom of my heart.

His stories are not just remarkable. They're remarkable in many ways. First, his fables about men and the Goddess illuminate women and men's relationships with each other. More, the writing *transforms* these relationships.

Yet there is more: Cohen addresses the human longing for Faerie tales with heroes. We have a real need for magical champions, but not male heroes who dominate. Daniel reveals the hero who instead *relates*.

Yet there is more: The tales are not just about gender and Deity; they are universal, touching the core of mysticism and freedom from dogma. The bard's job is to change the stories we tell, and thereby alter the entire pattern of how we live. Cohen deserves the title *bard*. His narratives need to be told and I, surely, need to hear them.

And there is more: Daniel's brain encompasses the enormity of details that comprise real life, so that he makes fine distinctions that other storytellers might miss. His understanding repeatedly makes me sigh with relief and recognition, and say, "Yes, yes, yes!"

Finally, Daniel is touched by something otherworldly. This makes me feel I am not alone as I adventure along meandering trails through far reaches of the cosmos.

Yes, when Daniel spins a tale, I laugh with joy at his mysticism and perceptive wit, sigh with relief, find healing through his gifts, and celebrate this fine storyteller.

Francesca De Grandis, author of *Bardic Alchemy: Enchanted Tales about the Quest for God/dess and Self*

DANIEL COHEN

INTRODUCTION
Surprising the Soul: the Secret of Stories

All myths central to a culture survive through a process of continual reinterpretation, satisfying the contradictory needs of individuals and society for images and narratives of both continuity and transformation. Vital myths are paradoxically both public and private, they encode both consent to and dissent from existing power structures, and they have at all times the potential for being interpreted both officially and subversively.
(Alicia Ostriker. *Feminist Revision and the Bible.* p. 28)

Pico believed it was important to surprise the soul through interpretations of images and stories. Since interpretation consists chiefly in discovering new images among the old, the surprise Mercury brings is a new image or a new idea, a gift from the cunning god who knows how to stir the soul.
(Thomas Moore. *Care of the Soul.* p. 152)

Stories form a prism through which we see the world.

We define our lives by the stories we tell ourselves and each other about our childhoods, friends, work, ambitions, and hopes. We may see ourselves as the golden child who can do no wrong or as a failure in whatever we do. In their emotional life, men may see themselves as Don Juan or Casanova, women as Cinderella looking for Prince Charming or as Beauty taming the Beast. We may create our own stories, or we may try to fit ourselves into old stories or into the stories told by our families (who may classify us as "the clever one" or "the artistic one" among our brothers and sisters).

We live in two worlds, the world of facts, which we call the real world, and the world of stories, which we call the world of imagination or fantasy. Many people think the world of imagination is unimportant. But there is no meaning in the world of facts. All meaning comes from the world of stories, which makes it supremely important.

As we share each other's stories, we learn about ourselves, and, even more importantly, about our connections with each other and our similarities and differences.

We learn, too, from publicly told stories, whether in novels, films, or even popular songs or in the older form of oral storytelling, which is experiencing a revival, though it had at one time almost died out.

Public stories help define our culture. They tell us what is permissible and what is not, what and who is admired, and how we wish to treat each other.

Old stories that have survived have great power, because they relate to matters that have remained important through many changes in society. That is why they have survived.

By changing the stories we tell we can change our understanding and behaviour. But do we have to find new stories or can we take the old stories and tell them in a different way?

Many people, especially devotees of Jung and Campbell, think that there is only one correct way of telling a myth or traditional tale.

But this isn't so. Authors as diverse as the fantasy writer Neil Gaiman and the scholar Wendy Doniger and others have pointed this out. Gaiman emphasises the ways each teller imposes their own personality and concerns on the telling, and the richness this gives to the stories. Doniger points out the social and political content of myths, which can be used both to support and to subvert the dominant patterns.

An extreme example of different ways of telling a story is shown in the folk-tale *The Fairy Midwife*. At one point in this story, a woman, after putting ointment on one eye, sees differently with the two eyes. With one eye she sees reality, with the other eye glamour. With one eye she sees a rich mansion, with the other a poor hut. But which of the mansion and the hut is reality and which is glamour? I've heard two versions of this story that contradict each other at this crucial point, and so give completely different accounts of the relationship between the two worlds.

The Greek myths are among the most well-known of the old stories to those cultures stemming from Europe — they are better known than more local myths. Because they have been known so widely for so long, there is a tendency to think of them as unchanging, as representing eternal truths. But even among those ancient myths, there are variant versions. Later versions of the stories can be even more different. The film *Troy*, released in 2004, is certainly not the story told in the Iliad, but it works on its own terms. Lesley Fitton (curator of Greek Bronze Age antiquities at the British Museum) says that the film-makers "are only following ancient precedent if they change the story to make dramatic sense to a contemporary audience."

The versions that have come down to us were the product of a particular culture at a particular time. In this culture men were becoming dominant over women, and the tales of gods, goddesses, and heroes reflect this. In some cases earlier forms of the myths are known, and in others we can dimly perceive earlier forms beneath the better-known versions.

When we retell the myths, we may keep close to them as they are most commonly known, we may attempt to uncover older versions, or we may look for completely new ways of telling the stories. When this is done, we learn not just from the new forms of the stories but from the contrasts between old and new tellings. If we are interested in changing the ways in which people relate, then new tellings can be a valuable tool.

Feminists have been looking at myths and folktales for many years now, unpacking patriarchal content and reversing it. I have found many of the feminist versions, for instance Suniti Namjoshi's *Feminist Fables*, both profound and funny.

However, those versions often left me feeling dissatisfied because there was no place for me in them. My guess is that the feminist response to my dissatisfaction is that the stories were not written for me, that if I wanted stories to which I could relate directly then I should write such stories myself. This is what I have done.

In my retellings, I bring insights from feminist spirituality and the Goddess movement to create new images of the hero, subverting the traditional images. These new images are transformative for both men and women, and for all our relationships to each other and to the natural world. They nourish and strengthen everyone seeking equality and an end to gender prejudice.

My stories are teaching tales. They are designed to support men in the work of finding non-oppressive ways of behaving, of employing talents and strengths to heal and not to harm, and to ensure that they do not take the path of denying their strengths and talents. As men look closely at them, I hope they will see new images of the hero, new — but perhaps also very old — ways of acting I also hope that these new images and suggestions of new behaviour will offer women an assurance that such changes are possible, and so help to heal the wounds caused by patriarchy and bring companionship and community.

And yet, though my stories are teaching tales, tools for change, I have considerable discomfort at the thought of stories as tools. To regard stories solely as tools is to devalue them. Many people think that problems in society can be resolved with the aid of stories. They regard a story as casting light on a dilemma, and so helping in its solution. My preference is to look at matters the other way round. Instead of saying that a problem can be resolved with the help of a story, I prefer to say that the problem provides an occasion on which the story can be told. And each such situation, with the problem and its resolution, provides a deepening of the story.

However, teaching is not the only purpose of my stories. I wrote them because they came bubbling up. Did they come through me because they wanted to teach? Certainly, the stories themselves insisted that they wanted to be heard, they would not stop calling on my attention until I wrote them down.

Stories like to be told. As these stories chose me to be their first teller, I have to honour their trust by producing this book. I am not the owner of the stories, they own themselves and have an independent life. To ensure that they, and their transformative possibilities, have as wide a circulation as possible, I give permission for others to retell them under the conditions noted on the copyright page

DANIEL COHEN

THE STORY OF THE STORY

In the beginning was the Story.

Some say it was the Word. But they are referring to that great creative power that changes everything it touches. Although Word is a good name for it, others have named it, with equal truth, as Music, Song, or Dance. So Story, which can include all these others, seems the best name.

And the Story realised that it needed a place in which to spread itself. So, in a rush of energy, it began to create particles, stars, galaxies. And then it went on to create planets, worlds full of mountains, rivers, seas, clouds.

Now that the Story had a place, it needed characters. So it created living beings, quick ones like may-flies, slow ones like turtles, huge ones like whales, tiny ones like lichen. And it woke up the spirits of what it had created earlier, rocks, rivers, winds, and even the planets and stars themselves. And it was not only on Earth that it created its characters. Nor was it only in the physical world that they existed. Dragons, vampires, elves, brownies, boggarts, and even Martians and hobbits found they were a part of the Story. And all these beings began to play their parts in the Story. Some of them — the humans were among those — began to sense parts of the Story and to tell parts to each other. And some even began to see that their lives were part of a story. A few sensed the existence of the Story itself, and realised that they were participants in this great Story.

In all the worlds stories were told and stories were lived. One story would be told or lived many times in many ways — sometimes the tellings of a single story would be so different that they seemed to have nothing in common, yet they were all forms of one story which was itself part of the great Story.

Here are some of the little stories that made up parts of the great Story. You may have come across some of these stories before, but you will not have met with these particular tellings elsewhere.

DANIEL COHEN

THE HEART OF THE LABYRINTH

This is how they tell the story.

They tell that the Minotaur was a monster, half man, half bull, who dwelt in the labyrinth. They tell that Theseus was a brave youth who determined to kill the Minotaur. They tell that Ariadne was a princess who fell in love with Theseus and gave him a thread to guide him. They tell that Theseus marched unfearingly into the labyrinth, braving the bellowing monster at its heart, and that he met the Minotaur and slew it. They tell that he emerged a great man who in later years won the love of many women and gloriously conquered many lands.

This is what they do not tell us.

They do not tell us that Theseus was afraid, but refused to acknowledge his fear. They do not tell us that as Theseus heard the Minotaur's bellows, he realised that they were songs, sometimes so sad that he wanted to weep, sometimes so joyful that he wanted to dance, but that he suppressed these feelings and marched on. They do not tell us that when he met the Minotaur he saw that the beast-man had his own features. They do not tell us that he was so enraged by this that he instantly killed the Minotaur. They do not tell us that, confident that nothing of the animal remained in him, he went on to rape many women, calling it love, and to kill many people, calling it glory.

This is how it was and still is and should not be.

DANIEL COHEN

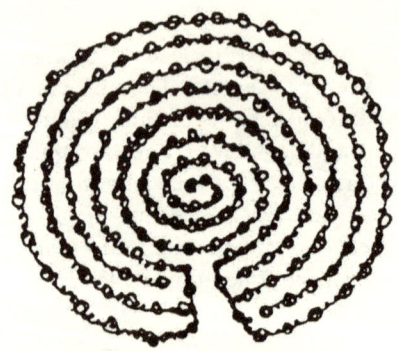

This is how it was in the deeper past and how it could be again.

Theseus knew it was time for him to enter the labyrinth and confront the Minotaur. He was afraid and so he asked the Goddess Ariadne for a token, as it was in her service and for love of her that he was going. She gave him a thread from her web, which is the world, to remind him that the dark labyrinth too was her realm, and that She who he loved could be found in darkness as in light. He entered the labyrinth, afraid of the Minotaur's bellowing but hopeful that he could do what was needed. As he moved in deeper he realised that the bellows were songs, sometimes so sad that he wept, sometimes so joyful that he danced. At the heart of the labyrinth he confronted the Minotaur and discovered that it had his own features. Joyfully he embraced his brother and they danced and sang, sometimes together, sometimes apart. Finally the handsome youth began his journey out of the labyrinth leaving the beast-man at its heart. He returned the thread to the Lady Ariadne who wove it once more into her web as a connection now between the ordinary world and the mysteries of the deep labyrinth. In the heart of the labyrinth Theseus remained until the time came round for the Minotaur to seek him once more.

THE LABYRINTH OF THE HEART

THE LABYRINTH OF THE HEART

FACE OF WISDOM, FACE OF DREAD

Many men had sought to kill the Gorgon Medusa, one of three sisters who men called monsters, only to be turned to stone when they caught sight of her terrible face with her hair formed of coiling snakes. The Goddess Athene called on the hero Perseus, saying "It is necessary that I have the head of Medusa. Therefore I bid you seek out Medusa for me."

Perseus answered "I will do this gladly. But where can I find Medusa? And is there any aid you can give me?" Athene replied "You may borrow my shield. It is brightly polished, so bright that it could act as a mirror as well as a shield. So that you may travel swiftly I have borrowed for you the winged sandals of Hermes, who journeys on them not only in this world, but also to the realms of the gods and even to the Underworld. You must find out the path to Medusa for yourself. But you should enquire of the Graiae, who dwell far off in the midst of Ocean. They share between them the Eye of the Seer and the Tooth of True Speech."

Perseus set out. He crossed many lands, met people whose ways appeared utterly strange to him and found that he appeared equally strange to them; he met beasts both beautiful and ugly, and saw that all behaved according to their nature. At last he reached the shores of Ocean, and prepared to travel above its waters till he found the island of the Graiae.

As he flew on he saw Ocean in all its changing moods. When the sun shone he saw the blue and green depths, so calm that birds nested on its surface and dolphins leapt from sea to air and fell back into the sea. He gloried in the wildness of the storms, when waves reached almost up to his feet and he saw the great Sea-Serpent lashing its coils. At one time he heard the Sirens singing and tried to go to them; fortunately his sandals refused to obey him.

Despite the winged sandals, his search took many days, and when at last he reached the island of the Graiae he was exhausted, unable to move further. He slumped down as he landed, and one of his sandals fell off into the sand. He searched for it, but was unable to find it and resolved to walk on despite having only one sandal.

He walked for some time, in his exhaustion doubling back and re-crossing his path many times before he found the Graiae. Those three strange women, who were old when they were born and had not aged in the many years since their birth, were passing between them the Eye and the Tooth. He asked them "Can you tell me how to find Medusa. The Goddess Athene has sent me, and she advised me to ask for your aid."

One replied "We will not tell you." He thought angrily how easy it would be to seize the Eye and the Tooth and force them to answer. He

13

considered doing this, since he could see no other way of getting the answer he needed. But he recalled also that Athene had told him to ask the Graiae, and had not in any way suggested he might have to use force. What would Athene want him to do? The long silence as he pondered what to do was broken when another of the Graiae said, "You may borrow the Eye. It will give you clear vision and you may see for yourself how to find Medusa", and the third said "You may borrow the Tooth, so that you can speak out the path."

Perseus looked long through the Eye, and he appeared dazed when he gave it back, as if its vision had been beyond his imaginings. "Back", he said, "back along my path to where I started the journey." "But," he added as he returned the Tooth, "if that is where Medusa is, why did Athene send me so far?"

One of the Graiae replied "Some have found the Gorgon without seeking us. But all of those have been turned to stone." Another said "Some have crossed Ocean and tried to force the secret from us. Nothing more has been heard of them — doubtless they too have become stone." The third went on "But some, like you, have observed Ocean as they travelled, and rejoiced at its wildness and mystery. They have spoken to us courteously. Those have been successful in their task, as you may well be."

"But if others have succeeded before me," said Perseus, feeling confused, "how is it that Medusa is still there?" "How, indeed?" came the answer. "Perhaps Medusa, like the Hydra, grows a new head each time." "Perhaps" said another "there is a different Medusa for each seeker."

"And perhaps" began the third, but she broke off when the other two glared at her as if she was giving away a secret. "Do you remember, young man," she went on, "what Athene said to you. For you will not succeed in your task unless you bear her words in mind." Perseus, casting his memory back, said "Why, she lent me her shield and the sandals of Hermes and demanded that I slay the Gorgon and bring her its head." "Did she," came the answer, "did she indeed? Well, young man, it is time for you to leave. Maybe, if you think hard, you will succeed."

Perseus walked back to the place where he had landed. After some searching he found the missing sandal, bound it on, and began retracing his path. He kept trying to recall Athene's words and trying to work out a way to kill Medusa without seeing her face. He remembered that Athene had told him the shield was as bright as a mirror and wondered if it would be safe to see only Medusa's reflection. He uncovered the shield and looked into it. He saw reflected the calm sea, the blue sky, the sun and his own figure. He thought how handsome he looked, how brave, how loving and how lovable.

THE LABYRINTH OF THE HEART

DANIEL COHEN

A cloud passed over the sun, the wind rose, and the waves began rising fiercely as the shield misted over. When it cleared he saw himself again with the angry elements reflected too. He saw how cruel he had been many times, how mean, how uncaring, how petty, how fearful.

He recalled how he had been about to threaten the Graiae to force answers from them. Force and threats had been his answer to so many problems. He saw in the shield the face of a woman he had once been attracted to. He was not her first choice, nor even her second, but he had driven his rivals away. One he had threatened with a beating if he did not leave. He had persuaded another man that she would be happier with a hero such as Perseus, and that his rival would give her up if he truly loved her. And once he had disposed of his rivals and won her, he soon tired of her, claiming that a hero had more important things to do than spend time with a woman.

His sandals brushed the tops of the waves and he felt it would be best for everyone if he let himself fall into the water.

But he remembered that Athene had given him a task and he contin0ued on. The shield misted and cleared once more. He now saw that both pictures were true, that he was a mix of many things, some of which he had never looked at before. He saw that in trying to present a heroic picture always, he was denying much of himself and becoming inhuman by trying to be superhuman. The sun shone, the wind was cold but refreshing, and the sea was choppy. In the distance ahead of him he could see black clouds and stormy seas that he would have to go through, but further on the skies were blue again.

As he continued back along his path he saw that the seasons had changed. It had been spring when he started, but now leaves had fallen and winter was beginning. He returned to the place where Athene had first spoken to him and noticed a cave on the hillside, which he felt sure was the Gorgon's home. He drew his sword, uncovered the shield and waited. A movement from the cave caught his eye, and involuntarily he glanced towards it. He caught a quick glimpse of Medusa's face, and his blood began to freeze. He stood still as a stone, feeling as if poisonous snakes were crawling all over him. He could think of nothing except how evil he was, unloving, cruel, fearful, not fit to be human, deserving only to be turned into stone as a warning to others.

With a great effort he moved slightly and caught sight of Athene's shield, with his own figure reflected in it. He recalled that he had seen similar images of himself in the shield, but had been shown that, though they were true, they were only part of the truth. He felt free to move and lifted his sword once more to kill Medusa. But as he moved he reflected and remembered the parting words of the Graiae. What had Athene's exact words been?

Still staring into the shield as if it could help him, he struggled to recall Athene's command before taking any action. At last he remembered and turned to face the Gorgon. He saw what Athene's carefully chosen words had meant. She had not commanded him to kill Medusa, but had bidden him to seek out Medusa, which he had done. She had said that it was necessary that she should have the head of Medusa, and indeed it was so. He knew why the Goddess Athene, Lady of reason and of the wisdom of the daylight, should, in that time and place, show herself as Medusa, the Lady of intuition and the wisdom of the night. The two were one, as they always had been. Athene had always had the head of Medusa as one of her aspects, and it was necessary, as she had said, that this was so.

MAIDEN AND MONSTER

Perseus flew on, away from Medusa, across the sea until he reached a rocky coastline, the boundary of a fertile kingdom. Here he landed and was given hospitality by the king and queen. Though they made him a welcome guest he could see that they were greatly upset and he asked why. He learnt that they had offended the Changeless Changeable Ones, the Goddesses of the Sea. They had sent out a sea-serpent and demanded that the princess Andromeda be given to the monster. The king and queen begged Perseus, who they could see was a hero, to aid them and he agreed.

Next morning Andromeda was taken to the seashore and chained to a rock. She asked them not to chain her, saying that it was not necessary and that the monster was her fate. But they were afraid she would run away and bring a worse disaster on the land, and they would not listen to her.

Perseus leapt lightly into the air on his winged sandals, while the king and queen and all the people retired to the safety of a cliff-top. Perseus looked at Andromeda as he waited for the monster — as she stood there so calmly the tall grey-eyed young woman seemed to him like a mortal image of Athene. He looked out to sea where great waves were coming in as the monster approached. The monster in some way reminded him of the Gorgon. He waited for the monster to come closer. The people on the cliff-top were cheering madly at the sight of him, encouraging him while he waited.

He continued to wait while the sea-beast came closer and closer. His mind whirled as he looked, now out to sea, now back to the shore. Andromeda... Athene... the monster... Medusa... Andromeda... the monster... Athene... Medusa. As the monster neared the shore he drew his sword. The crowds on the cliff-top were calling even more wildly now, yelling "Strike", "Save the princess", "Kill the monster" and other encouragements. He raised his sword and struck downwards swiftly and accurately.

The sword cut keenly through the chains binding Andromeda. She walked calmly across to the waiting beast, stroked it, climbed onto its back, and the two sped out to sea and were soon lost to sight. Before she left she gave Perseus a smile of thanks.

But he realised that the thanks were due from him to her. She had known that the monster was her destined ally who would help her find the freedom she sought. She could simply have waited for the monster to break the chains, but she chose to give Perseus the opportunity to make a good decision. He was glad she was prepared to trust in him and wondered what would have happened if he had killed the monster.

DANIEL COHEN

Perhaps Andromeda, whose name — which meant 'ruler of men' — suggested her destiny, would have become bound to him by invisible chains more imprisoning than those he had cut. Perhaps she would be known only as "the rescued princess" or "the wife of Perseus", and not recognised as a person in her own right. Perhaps he would have come to seem to her, and even to be, more frightening than any monster, a cruel being who could only destroy, not create.

CIRCE'S BARD

You have heard of the exploits of Odysseus. You will recall how he landed on Circe's island. You remember that many of his men went up to Circe's palace, and that she gave them food and drink, but after that she changed them into swine. Odysseus went searching for his men. On his way he met the god Hermes, who gave him the plant moly as a protection, and so he was able to free his men. But the poet chose not to tell part of the tale, because it meant too much to him. It is that part which I tell now.

Odysseus brought a bard with him on his journeys. He was not a particularly good bard, but he was good enough to know what a true bard is like. Not that Odysseus ever noticed the quality of his bard. He had no great respect for bards. They were in his view not people of any significance; just useful servants who could keep the men cheerful and encourage them to fight. It was now the fashion for kings to keep one or two bards, and this was supposed to add to the royal dignity; but no serious-minded practical person really considered bards were important. This was Odysseus' opinion, though he was careful not to state such unfashionable views aloud.

Now this bard was among the men who went towards Circe's palace. But he was soon left behind by the others, because he was taking time to look around in the hope that he would gain ideas for a new song. So he was by himself when the god Hermes appeared to him, and said (as he was later to say to Odysseus) "This island belongs to Circe. If you take this plant called moly and keep it next to your heart it will protect you from Circe's enchantments." The bard gave thanks and took the plant.

Then Hermes said, "I had not expected that a bard would choose to take this plant." To this the bard replied "It is never wise to refuse the gifts of the Gods. But how we choose to use them is another matter."

Hermes smilingly said, "I see you know something of the trickster's art. Therefore go with my blessing."

When the bard reached Circe's palace, he could see nothing of his companions, but Circe assured him they were happy, and so he was content to eat. At the end of a magnificent meal, she offered him spiced wine, which had been mulling in a white cauldron. Before drinking it, he took out the moly and offered it to her with these words. "This herb is black at the root and white in the flower. It signifies the union of night and day in holy love. A plant with such rare qualities is a gift fitting for Circe, who holds both the wisdom of the day and that of the night."

Taking the plant, Circe crushed it into the wine and again offered it to him. He drank, and was immediately filled with wisdom and understanding. He became aware of all the secrets on the earth, above it, and below it, of the nature of all things, living and non-living, and he found that at last his abilities as a bard were such as he had always known were possible.

Circe smiled at him. In her smile he saw the unity of all beings. He understood that she changed men into animals that they might realise this themselves. The hunter and the hunted were alike part of the unity, and each of these was a form she took. In her honour, and almost without conscious thought, he changed himself into a stag. He left the palace and ran to the surrounding woods. Here he roamed for some time. He gradually realised that the drink he had taken had given him great understanding of the earth, the trees and plants, and all animals and all beings that dwelt on the earth, and yet his understanding was now greater, since it was coupled with experience. But after a while he began to feel a presence behind him, and a sense of danger. Looking around, he saw that he was being pursued by a she-wolf. He ran and dodged, but the wolf continued to follow him, coming ever closer. By the time he had reached the shore, the wolf was almost on him, and he ran into the water with the wolf still on his heels.

Once in the water, he escaped from the wolf by changing into a mullet. He swam for some time, investigating the element in which he found himself. He gradually realised that the drink he had taken had given him great understanding of the waters, both salt and fresh, and of all beings that dwelt in the waters, and yet his understanding was now greater, since it was coupled with experience. But after a while he began to feel a presence behind him, and a sense of danger. Looking round, he saw that he was being pursued by a dolphin. He swam and dodged, but the dolphin continued to follow him, coming ever closer. After a while the dolphin was almost on him, and he made a great leap into the air.

Once in the air, he changed into a dove. He gradually realised that the drink he had taken had given him great understanding of the air, its winds both great and small, its birds and insects, and of all beings that dwelt in the air, and yet his understanding was now greater, since it was coupled with experience. But after a while he began to feel a presence behind him, and a sense of danger. Looking round, he saw that he was being pursued by a hawk. He turned and dodged, but the hawk continued to follow him, coming ever closer. After a while the hawk was almost on him. As she made ready to dive on him, he made straight for a heap of corn that lay on the ground beneath him.

THE LABYRINTH OF THE HEART

Once among the corn, he changed into a grain of corn. He gradually realised that the drink he had taken had given him great understanding of fire, both the fires of the sun and the fires of the earth, and of the fiery spirit that impelled all beings. Yet his understanding was now greater, since it was coupled with experience. But after a while he began to feel a presence near him, and a sense of danger. He heard a scratching, and became aware that a black hen was searching through the corn for him. He realised that to do what was necessary this time would take all his wisdom and all his courage and all his strength.

Summoning up all his powers, he remained still as the hen came nearer and nearer. Finally, with a triumphant peck, she swallowed him.

When Odysseus came, he freed his men. Noticing that the bard was not among them, he demanded to know from Circe what had happened to him. But she replied that the bard was in human form, in a place of his own choosing from which he would emerge at the time most suitable, and that any attempt to bring him out sooner would only harm him. Since she swore by the Styx that this was so, which is an oath that binds even the gods and goddesses, Odysseus accepted her word and left the island without the bard.

And so, in due course, Circe gave birth to a son. He was a fine child, and she was glad to share her wisdom with him. Indeed, it seemed as if she was not teaching him, but only reminding him of what he already knew. His inner sight was all the more powerful because his outer sight was lacking — he was born blind. His lack of sight made sound and language especially important to him. Perhaps it was for this reason that poetry and music came so easily to him, or perhaps they too were reminders of what he had always known.

When the child was old enough, she sent him away from her island to make his way in the world. At first he sang in taverns for a few small copper coins. But gradually people began to feel that his songs were out of the ordinary. His reputation grew, and he was asked to perform in many places. He was glad to sing before the great lords and ladies, but he was just as glad to perform in the market-places. All he asked for was that his listeners paid him the courtesy of their full attention, and indeed this happened more often when he told tales old and new in the market-place than when he sang in the courts.

His songs in honour of the gods and goddesses are still known to us today. Although Odysseus thought little of bards, the name of Odysseus is now remembered only because of the tales told by the man who was given birth to by Circe.

THE FERRYMAN

Would I like a change from poling this ferryboat? No, sir, I would not, and you folks wouldn't like it if I did change. Why wouldn't you like it? I was created for this job when the first human being came into existence, and I'll continue in it till the last human dies — the way you people go on that may not be long.

Yes, many people do think they are going to go a different way, but they all take this boat in the end. What about near-death experiences? Those people may have been near Death, but they hadn't got far enough to be anywhere near me.

Do I mind that they used to bring money for me but have stopped doing so? No, sir, I do not mind — that was just their own idea, that all ferrymen should be paid. Still, it was a nice thought, but they might have considered that there was nowhere for me to spend the money. In fact, getting rid of it used to be a bit of a bother.

What's it like over there? I've never stopped on the far shore long enough to find out. But the Warrior — you know, the one who fought in that great Ten Years' War, said "I would rather be the meanest slave on earth than rule in this land."

Am I finding the job more difficult with so many souls to ferry across? No, souls weigh nothing, so the boat isn't burdened. Mind you, they did try a modern paddle-boat once so as to take more across at one time. But that kept breaking down once it was halfway across, and I had to come to the rescue. They soon decided that my old reliable arms on the pole were better than steam or any other mechanism.

Isn't it crowded over there with so many souls? It isn't the kind of place that gets crowded. Mind you, I have heard that there's another river and another ferryman who takes them back into the world sooner or later. But, of course, that's only what I've heard — I haven't seen for myself.

Did I know you were still alive? Of course I did — look how the boat is weighed down. Over the years I've come to know when a living person is on the boat. I could tell you a lot about some of them.

You'd like to hear some of those stories? Maybe you know them already, but you'll get more details from me. There was that musician. He played so fine as we crossed that the journey was faster and easier than usual. He came looking for his lost lady-love, and asked the Queen to send her back. But he was such a fool that he didn't recognise her when he saw Her, so he lost her again.

Then there was that Athenian apology for a hero — the one who got the Cretan princess to fall in love with him, help him, and go away with him, and who then abandoned her. He and a friend of his turned up at the boat landing roaring drunk. High and mighty they were — laughed at me behind their hands, made jokes about me they thought I was too stupid to understand, and called me a rude mechanical. They came over to see if the Queen fancied them. She wouldn't have minded that — She might even have responded — but they were so full of themselves that they were quite prepared to rape her. That Athenian said that he'd carried off the Amazon queen and she'd learned to love him in the end (little he knew!) and he didn't see why the Queen was any different. Naturally, She was very annoyed and put them in a really nasty place.

In the end, the Big Man came here and rescued them. The Big Man? You know, the strong one who did all those tasks. He wasn't very bright — tended to think that killing something was a good solution to problems. But whatever he did, even when it was a mistake, he did for love of Her and to Her glory. That's why She was willing to let those two go when he asked Her.

He was a real gentleman, the Big Man. When he came on my boat, he saw that I was really struggling with his weight. So he took a hand at the pole himself. Kind of him, and brave too. Brave? He couldn't be sure that I wouldn't jump off at the landing, and leave him to pole the boat forever. You think that wouldn't have occurred to him. It would — there was a time when he'd almost been caught by a similar trick.

Bless you, sir, that wasn't a hint. Nice of you to think of it, but you really wouldn't do well with the pole, so long and heavy as it is, would you, sir? You look more of an intellectual than an active type.

You say you want to know about other living people who've been and come back? There've been a few through the centuries. Would I tell you about them? No, sir, those later ones mostly didn't talk about it at all, and I'm not one to betray confidences.

Well, here we are at the landing. Jump out, sir. Would I be prepared to take you back? No, sir, I would not — that's not how I work. If I do, you'll write about me? Very civil of you, sir, but the answer's still no. I took those others back? Yes, sir, but they'd been to see Her, and got Her permission to come back.

Just follow that path, sir, until you get to Her palace, and ask Her. Will She give you permission? I don't know, sir. She might well. She likes those who are willing to risk the danger of the journey just to do Her honour.

You can never be sure, though. She's changeable in Her ways. She is power, love, justice, mercy, and also rage, anger, sometimes even despair and misery, and more besides. She once said, "I am all that is, was, and ever will be." Yes, sir, that does mean that you and I are just parts of Her if we only knew it — so is this boat, and the dolphins you folk talk about so much nowadays — for that, matter, so are those mosquitoes you curse, and even those nasty new weapons of yours.

THE LABYRINTH OF THE HEART

She wants you to face Her, even when you don't know what mood She's in. She's not going to make it easy for people — they have to come to Her with love for all Her moods, and be willing to risk not being allowed back.

Watch out for that big black dog of Hers, though. He's fierce, and tries to stop people getting past and reaching Her. You've brought some steak for him, have you? So when you asked me to ferry you back directly, that was just a joke — you knew all along that once you start this journey there's no going back until you've been face-to-face with Her.

It's been a pleasure talking to me? It's been a pleasure talking to you, sir. I hope to see you again for a return trip before too long. Good luck, sir.

THE LABYRINTH OF THE HEART

THE BIGGEST DUNG-HEAP IN THE WORLD

Heracles was condemned by the gods to perform twelve great labours. The fifth of these was to clean out the stables of King Augeas. Not a task for a hero, you might think, or one worthy of remembrance. But these were no ordinary stables. Augeas had been blessed and his flocks and herds had prospered for many years. It had been prophesied that his land would diminish if the dung were ever removed and so it had been left to accumulate over the years.

Finally the stench grew too great; the palace became uninhabitable and clouds of flies brought pestilence over the country. King Augeas resolved that the dung must be cleared despite the prophecy. But the men he first employed soon fell sick, and he sought advice from the oracle, who replied "Honour the glory of Hera, and all will be well."

The king made many sacrifices to the goddess Hera, but the pestilence continued. He realised that he had to look further at the oracle's words, to see what other meaning they could have. As he was thinking, word came to him that the hero Heracles was at the palace claiming guest-right. Augeas knew that the name 'Heracles' meant 'Glory of Hera' and resolved to treat him as more than a guest, more even than a hero, but as the one destined to cure the evils that were besetting the land.

Next day Augeas explained his troubles, and Heracles agreed to help. He began by clearing some of the dung from the stinking stables to the yard nearby. Though the air and the sun dispersed some of the odours, it was soon clear that this was no solution and that the mass of dung could not remain in one place. So he began taking it to the fields and spreading it around, and finally digging it into the ground so that the smell was no longer present. Even for Heracles, who was the strongest man of all time, this was not an easy or a pleasant task. By the third day he thought the stench would be with him for ever, no matter how many times he bathed, and that soon he would not be able to see a fly without screaming, as he had been surrounded by flies buzzing and landing on him throughout his labour.

Then a clever man came to him. The man said, "It will take many days to clear the dung the way you are doing. I have a better idea. There is a river nearby. It would be no great task for you to cut a channel so that the river flows through the stables and washes them out."

Heracles thought this was a brilliant idea. He began to cut the channel, rejoicing that he no longer had flies all around him. As he dug he looked at the river, seeing how it sparkled, and how water-weeds grew and fish swam. He remembered the sewers he had seen, and how nothing seemed to live in them. He began to wonder what would happen to the river if he followed the clever man's plan. He worked slower and slower and finally dropped his spade and returned to his old way of clearing the stables, dedicating his unpleasant work, as he did his whole life, to the glory of Hera.

The clever man left, mocking Heracles. When he returned to his own country, he told everyone what a clever idea he had had, and how foolish Heracles was not to follow the suggestion. He told the tale so often that in later years it was believed that Heracles had followed this plan. But that was many years later, when the clever man's people had left their country; their land was no longer fertile enough to feed the people, although the clever man and his clever friends kept thinking of ever more ingenious plans to restore fertility. Meanwhile Heracles had finished clearing the stables and digging dung deep into the earth throughout the fields of King Augeas's country. The dung had been removed from the stables but not from the land, and King Augeas and his country continued to prosper.

HAPPY THE LAND THAT NEEDS NO HEROES

We are blind now, my sisters and I.

He came to us, the hero, the shining one, Perseus, proud in his strength, bright as the two lightning flashes on his tunic.

There were three of us, three sisters known as the Graiae. We had always had only one eye between us, which we passed from one to another, yet we saw more clearly with that one eye between three than many did with two eyes to themselves.

And we saw him for what he truly was.

"Where is she," he demanded.

" Who," I asked, though we knew well what it was he wanted.

"Medusa. She whose snakes creep in and poison our good and wholesome society."

We laughed at the way he saw the world, and I answered "No." I spoke for us all, since at the time I had our one tooth.

But then I made a mistake. Wishing my sisters to see him, I took out the eye so as to pass it to one of them. But he grabbed the eye as I tried to hand it on.

"Now you will tell me," he said triumphantly, holding the eye tight in his hand.

"No." At that, he began to squeeze the eye in his fist. We all felt the pain.

"Tell me, or else"

"No." He squeezed the eye more. The pain was intense.

"Tell me where Medusa is." "No." Another squeeze. More pain.

"Tell me." "No." Squeeze. Pain. "Tell me." "No." Squeeze. Pain.

The pain was almost unendurable. But it seemed that our determination not to reveal where our comrade was only grew stronger as the pain increased.

"Then take the consequences." He crushed the eye in his fist, and strode off.

We are blind now, my sisters and I. But our dear Medusa is still free. And though the tyranny of the strong still remains, it is not secure while her serpents remind the oppressed of their power when joined together.

Though we can no longer see the outside world, our inner vision has only been strengthened. And we see into the future. We mourn for and honour all those who remained faithful under torture. There are those whose names we see and many others whose names we do not know. You may recall some from near your own times — if you do not, then search out names, both to honour them and to give yourselves courage.

DANIEL COHEN

We also mourn for and honour those who resisted torture to the limit of their ability, but who found the pain too much and gave in. They did what they could — no-one knows their own limits until they are tested. We will not judge them.

And we remind you who live in future times that tyranny can appear pleasant if one is not suffering personally. It can appear as security and strength, as a barrier against the unknown, as liberation from the pains of the world. And even a good cause can turn into tyranny if the passion of its followers becomes too strong.

We are blind now, my sisters and I. You, the sighted ones, do not let yourself be dazzled by strength and beauty, but see tyranny and oppression for what they are. And, for as long as you can, resist.

DANIEL COHEN

THE FIRST CASUALTY OF WAR

This is the tale of the first death in the Trojan War.

The Greek army was gathered in Aulis. Its men had come from many towns and islands. Some were there with dreams of glory, some with dreams of gold. Others were there because their chief had demanded their presence, and either loyalty to the chief or fear of him had brought them.

The fleet was waiting and the soldiers were ready to embark. But for weeks now the wind had been blowing from the wrong direction, and the men were getting restless at waiting so long. They were beginning to think of the harvest — they had expected that the war would be won long before harvest time — but that was now so close that many men were making ready to go home, and some had already gone.

Agamemnon, the leader of the Greek army, was fearful that the conquest and glory he sought would escape him if the winds continued contrary. And so he consulted the seer Calchas. After much searching the seer replied, "The goddess Artemis sends you a warning. If you wish to make war against Troy, you will have to kill your daughter."

So Agamemnon sent for his daughter Iphigenia, pretending to her and her mother that he planned to marry her to the hero Achilles. When she arrived an altar was built to Artemis, and she was bound to the altar. Her mother, Clytemnestra, pleaded with Agamemnon for the life of their child, but he would not listen. Agamemnon raised the sacrificial knife, but as it descended a mist came down. When the mist cleared, Iphigenia had vanished, and a deer lay sacrificed on the altar. Shortly after, the wind changed, and the army set sail for Troy, but the rest of that tale is not part of our story.

So now you know who was the first to die in the war of the Greeks against Troy. But "No", you reply, "I had thought it would be Iphigenia, but since she vanished I have no idea who it can be." Do you truly have no idea? Then I will give you a clue.

Agamemnon would not listen to the pleas of his wife and daughter. He persisted in his plan to sacrifice his daughter, regardless of what her murder would do to his family and himself, regardless of what war would do to others. He thought of himself as a great man, he thought that a great man should look only to his own fame and ignore others, he thought that compassion was fit only for women and was no concern of his.

When this tale is told nowadays, men talk in horrified tones of the old bloodthirsty goddesses, of Artemis who demanded that Agamemnon sacrifice his daughter. They do not see that Artemis demanded no sacrifice. She simply gave Agamemnon a warning, that his acts would have consequences. The goddess tried to make him understand that the cost of his glory and fame was the death of many daughters and mothers, sons and fathers. That is why she asked if he was prepared to bring death to his own daughter.

Do you think Artemis should have spoken more clearly? The Immortals' desire for us is that we choose our own paths. They may warn or advise, but will not tell us what to do.

Now do you see who it was who first died? Surely those women who meet this tale know the answer by now. For you men who still do not know I will give one further clue. Even this clue may not be enough. You have the answer hidden deep within you. It may not yet be your time to become aware of it, but it is surely time to try.

Look into yourself — look into your heart. Do you see who it is who lies there, in a sleep near to death, a sleep that has lasted for centuries, a sleep from which only you can awaken her? Now do you know the answer to my question? Do you know? Do you?

(Some answers that others have given can be found in the notes to this story.)

DANIEL COHEN

THE SLEEPING BEAUTY

This is the tale of a quest. It is a tale for men. There is also a tale for women, but I am not the one to tell that tale. Women who come across this tale may ignore it or observe it, help or hinder the hero as they please.

It is a tale that may happen to you, as it has happened in its various ways to many men before you and will happen to many after you. It begins when you have a dream — or rather, a vision, for it is more real than any dream. You see a maiden in a castle surrounded by a barrier of thorns, a maiden who has been asleep for centuries. You learn that the spell which has imprisoned her was cast many generations ago by one of your forefathers. You resolve to find that castle and awaken the maiden, for you realise that she will not be freed unless you attempt that task, and that you must start at once or else you will be too late.

And so you set out. Many are the perils that men have encountered on such a journey, and many are the miracles, too. Perhaps you have to cross a trackless desert, or climb a mountain of glass. How have you treated those you met, whether stronger or weaker than you? Have you shared your food, have you treated the animals you met as beings with knowledge as valuable as yours? Perhaps you have helped others because it is in your nature — perhaps it is not in your nature, but you have nonetheless done so because you know it is right. Which of these two is more pleasing I do not know. Some say only the first will do, the other being no more than what one has learned is useful; others claim there is no credit in what comes naturally, and that choosing to do what is difficult must be what counts.

You have faced many perils, perils that have destroyed some and led others to retreat home. You have passed through them with the aid of those you have helped, perhaps not even being aware that the perils were there. You have come by grace or by luck — which some say is just another word for grace — to the edge of the lands surrounding the castle.

Here you find the way to the castle is barred by an immense growth of brambles and thorn bushes. Perhaps you expect that a way will open up before you, as you are the destined saviour of the maiden. If so, you are disappointed. If you push forward boldly, hacking at all the thorns with your sword or axe, it soon becomes blunted. If, being a modern man, you chose instead a flame-thrower to destroy the thorns, you find its power has died before you have got far. Tools do not help you, and you must find another way.

If you search closely, you will see the remains of a path, and notice that the bushes are less thick near it. As you follow the path it twists and turns, perhaps going backwards for a while. At times you have to stoop or even crawl, and sometimes you have to clear away some of the bushes where they are too thick to make progress, though usually you accept those scratches you receive. And at last, tired and scratched, you arrive at the clear ground in front of the castle.

You enter the castle, and make your way to the room where the maiden lies sleeping. Remembering old stories, you kiss her in the hope that the kiss will bring her back to life. Great is your joy as she wakes up and stands to greet you. But your joy turns to terror, for she has been asleep for centuries and now she is awake those centuries show on her: with each second she seems a year older until you are facing a woman older than you thought was possible.

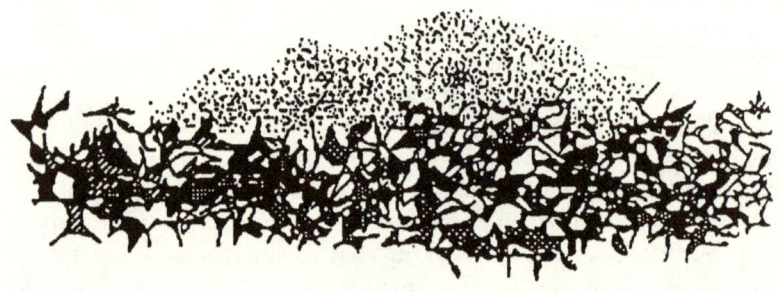

What do you do now? This is your tale, and I cannot answer that for you. But I can tell you what happened to others. Many, in their terror, rushed away from the castle, pushed their way through the thorns heedless of the deep scratches, and returned to the ordinary world. There were some who shut out their terror by denying that they ever made such a journey, while others bitterly regretted their faint-heartedness and spent much of their lives searching for a way back. I do not know if any of those ever found their way back; many of them spent so much time searching that the rest of life made no impression on them.

If you are one of those who remained, you will see that the woman is not only older than you thought possible, but also wiser than you thought possible and more fearsome than you thought possible. As she looks at you it seems to you that she is weighing up every action you have ever taken, every thought you have ever had, and will deliver her judgement. It may be that now is the time you choose to run away.

Or perhaps you realise that, though it was a maiden you came in search of, this woman, frightening as she seems, is still the one you sought. If you see this and remain, she changes yet again. Neither a maiden nor an aged woman, she becomes now a woman of your own age, full of strength and majesty and love. Many have reached the maiden, and few of those remained to face the old woman. Few even of those can face her now, and it may be now that you run away. For what she demands of you is nothing less than strength, majesty and love to equal her own, a thing you find harder even than facing the judgement of the old woman.

If you remain and reach out your hand to her, she takes it. Together you leave the castle of vision to live together in the world outside. "And the story ends," I hear you say thankfully, "as all good stories should, with the words 'And they lived happily ever after.'" Of course not! This is not a story told to pass the time when the TV is broken — it is a tale of reality. But I can promise you that if you have succeeded in coming this far then you will live more fully until your death, experiencing the joyousness of your joys, the sadness of your sorrows, the wrath of your angers, the pain of your hurts, and that you will never lose (though you may need to forget for a while) the knowledge of the world's waking beauty.

DANIEL COHEN

WHAT WOMEN MOST DESIRE

You have heard of King Arthur's knights, the Knights of the Round Table. You have heard how they fought in the cause of justice, protecting the weak against those who would oppress them. You may have learned that Lancelot was the best of those knights, though his love for Arthur's queen, Guenevere, led through the schemings of others to the destruction of Arthur's kingdom. Perhaps you have dreamed of yourself as Lancelot.

In older times there was another knight who was thought of as the best, until the later tales diminished him in favour of Lancelot. Here is part of his story.

That knight was Gawain. Gawain, Arthur's nephew; Gawain, sometimes named Gwalchmai, the Hawk of May; Gawain of the red hair and sunny disposition. Gawain, the only knight brave enough to play the beheading game with the Green Knight (though it is not of the Green Knight that I will tell today). It is Gawain who is the one of the Knights of the Round Table that I most admire; for me Lancelot is too remote. And now I tell how Gawain found his true love, and how, through no fault of his but through the pains of the natural world which we inhabit, he lost her.

King Arthur was riding alone in the forest one day, when a knight in black armour suddenly attacked him. Arthur, though he had his sword Excalibur and was a brave fighter, was after many struggles, defeated by the Black Knight. The Black Knight said, "You are my prisoner, and I could well hold you for ransom. But, since you are the king, I will give you one chance. I will ask you a question, and you may depart. If, in the course of a year, you can find the answer then you are free; if not, you must swear that you will give yourself up as my prisoner once more."

Arthur agreed — indeed, he had little choice — and the knight asked him, "Tell me, then, what is it that women most desire?"

And so, at dinner in the court that night, Arthur told of his adventure, and said to Guenevere, "Tell me, my dear, what is it that women most desire." Guenevere replied "A brave and handsome man to love them", looking at Arthur, though some said she was casting her eyes on Lancelot. Though many of the knights cheered at this, one of the ladies said "What is life without children?" and soon more and more answers came from various court ladies.

At length Gawain said that he would quest in search of the answer. Gawain was the knight who was most fitted for such a quest, for he (unlike many others of the Round Table, despite their virtues) was always courteous to ladies, and so they enjoyed his company, and on this quest he was the one to whom they would speak what was on their minds.

THE LABYRINTH OF THE HEART

So Gawain set out. He gathered many answers, until it seemed that there were as many answers as there were women he had asked. For, to one who said "What is life without children?" there was another who said "If only I did not have this brood of children", to one who said "I wish for a husband" there was another who said "If only I were not tied to this husband of mine", to one who said "If only I had something to do with my time" there was another who said "If only I was allowed to rest", to the one who said "If only I were grown-up" there was another who said "If only I were a child again". Gawain asked all the women he met; highborn ladies of the court, servants, housewives, goose-girls, hen-wives, young and old, high and low. Gawain was the one knight worthy of this quest; he alone was willing to ask of every woman, unlike other knights who would have regarded it beneath their dignity to ask of peasants or children; indeed, many of them would not even have noticed that these too were women who had desires of their own.

At last, with the year nearly at an end, Gawain rode home sadly, for none of the answers he had received seemed the right one. Suddenly, as he rode through a forest, a voice called out "Good day, Sir Gawain, why so sad?" He looked around, and saw a woman step out from behind a tree.

Or was it a woman? She seemed to him a figure out of nightmare, all his worst fears about age and deformity and illness and ugliness come true. Even Gawain, despite his courtesy to women, and though he had met women of many different shapes and ages on his journeys, shuddered and prepared to ride on.

But when she said again "Good day, Sir Gawain", he replied, with all the courtesy he could summon up, "Good day, lady. I have been on a quest, and am returning to Camelot, having failed in my quest."

"Not so," she replied, "There is still one day left, and I know the answer you seek to the question."

"Many women have given me answers, and none seems the true one," said he, not believing she could have the answer.

"Ah, but the answers you have been given were the answers of women's minds. I know the answer that lies in their hearts."

"Then, Lady, I pray you give me the answer."

"I will do so only if you give me what I ask."

"You may have whatever you ask for, if it be something which I may honourably give you."

"So, then, here is the answer to your question." (You who meet this story must wait a while to find out the answer.)

"Why, that sounds like the true answer. What boon do you desire?"

"I will come to Camelot after Arthur has answered the knight's question, and then I will claim my reward from you."

DANIEL COHEN

Gawain returned to Camelot, and gave the answer to the king. The Black Knight swaggered into the court, confident that he was the only man who knew the answer to his question, for he had tricked it (or so he thought) from the wise woman long ago. And he departed the court, angry but defeated, when King Arthur answered him. (No, this is not yet the time to reveal the answer.)

Arthur, Guinevere, and all the court sat down to feast and rejoice. But then the doors blew open, and in stepped the woman Gawain had met in the forest. It seemed as if a dark cloud had covered the sun, and all began to shiver.

"Now, Sir Gawain, you have seen that my answer was true, and I have come for my reward. I claim your hand in marriage."

The court shrank back in disgust, and everyone declared that this was a demand that should not be granted. But Gawain insisted that he was free to marry, that he could honourably do so, and that he had promised her anything that he could honourably do.

And so preparations for a wedding took place. But there was no joy in the court over this, and it seemed that more than one knight or lady was about to object when the priest asked if anyone knew of a reason why they should not be married. When the musicians began to play, and the bride called her husband to the dance, none were willing to join them in dancing.

At last the newly wedded couple retired to their room. They undressed and went to bed, though Gawain slunk as far from his bride as the bed would allow. But she said "Come, husband, I am your true wife, and I wish to be kissed and made love to as any woman would wish from the man she loves." So Gawain, though he found he could barely stand his bride's appearance and smell, and he remembered other ladies with whom he had gladly shared the pleasures of love, responded to his wife as he was in honour bound to do.

They then slept, with his arms around her as she desired. When he woke, he was amazed to find that he was clasping a young and beautiful maiden.

"Who are you?" he exclaimed.

"I am your wife, transformed by your courtesy from the shape in which you first saw me. But I cannot hold this shape always. Therefore tell me, shall I be like this at night and as you first saw me during the day, or shall I be like this in the day but as you first saw me at night."

"Why," was his first response, "Would not all men wish for beauty to make love to in the night?"

"If this is your choice, how long can you stand the laughter or pity of your fellow knights and the ladies of the court, for they will only see the hag you were forced into marrying."

"Well, then, it would seem that I must have you beautiful in the day."

"Aye, then, your comrades will envy you. But will you be content, even for a short while, to have to make love to one such as I was. Now, Gawain, you must choose. Choose carefully, for your future depends on it."

"This question is too deep for me. And, though you say that my future depends on my choice, it seems to me that it is your future that the decision affects, even more than mine. Therefore do you, my lady wife, choose as you think best."

And then Gawain's eyes misted over, and he could no longer see his wife clearly. When his vision returned, she had changed again. She was more beautiful than before, more mature, wiser. In another form she had answered the Black Knight's question, and had deep answers to many questions. It seemed to him that the wisdom of that hag was hers and yet also the joy in living of the maiden. "Ah, Gawain," she smiled "I see that you have learned my lesson well. Instead of you deciding for me, I have had my own will in that which concerns me. That, indeed, is what women most desire."

And so Gawain and his lady lived happily for several years, and great was their joy when, at the end of five years, she became pregnant. It seemed to them that a child was to be the culmination of their joy.

But it was not to be. Gawain's joy turned to sorrow when his wife died in childbirth.

So Gawain became once more a knight-errant, refusing to spend time at court, since it reminded him of his lost love. He became even more famous, and loved by those who were not knights. When there was oppression, when those with power attempted to get their way without thinking of others, he was the one of the Knights of the Round Table who was first in combating injustice.

Since he fought so often, he had many wounds. And in his conquests, though he was merciful, there were those he had to kill if he was to live. Yet it always seemed to him worth risking death that a peaceful and free kingdom could survive.

But there were times when his mourning for his lady almost overwhelmed him. It was then that he realised that his risking death was a great thing, but that there was a greater that he could barely begin to understand. In the world he wished to see, there would no longer be a need for men to risk their lives in combat. For women risked their lives too, in a cause better than his, and would still do so, even in a peaceful world. Like his love, many of them faced death and some died, not that the world should be better but for a deeper reason, for life itself. When he

THE LABYRINTH OF THE HEART

struggled, there were times when he brought death. But the women who faced death in their struggles brought new life.

And in later years, the stories told of Gawain as a great lover of women. Though this was true, few of the tellers knew that Gawain loved women deeply, not solely for their physical charms (as indeed he had shown when he won his bride by courtesy to one he found loathsome), but because he saw that they could be braver than the bravest knight.

DANIEL COHEN

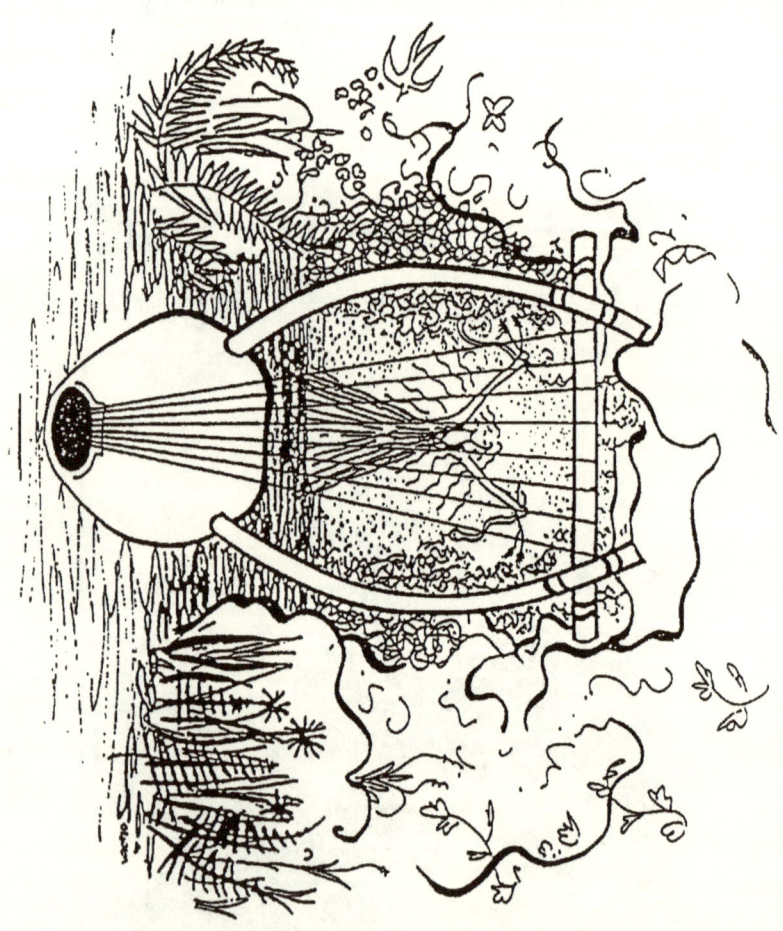

THE LABYRINTH OF THE HEART

THE SINGER'S LOST LOVE

Once there was a singer. Some said he was the finest singer that ever lived. And indeed his tunes were marvellous. Once he had escaped from wild beasts by playing and singing to them a quiet tune until they drifted to sleep. He had dispelled a snowstorm by singing of his delight in the hot days of summer. It was even said that once the rhythms of the dance he was playing were so lively that the trees themselves lifted up their roots to join in.

In time he met a maiden and they fell in love. Together they wandered, and all his songs were songs of joy and in praise of her. As he played and she danced, flowers sprung up behind them, and it seemed as if all the world shared in their joy. The skies were blue, the sun was hot, and from time to time they were refreshed by showers.

All went well until one day they saw an empty snakeskin on the path. The singer shuddered, for he was reminded of poison and death. But his love was delighted by the snakeskin, picked it up and showed him how it reflected the light and took on many colours, and how the snake had grown and left its unwanted skin behind to give others pleasure. He would not listen, and closed his eyes and put his hands over his ears trying to shut out what he could not understand.

That night they went to sleep as usual, but when he awoke in the morning she was not there. He looked for her, thinking she was teasing him and was not far away. After a time he became worried and sung loudly to call her back in case she had lost her way. When he realised she had truly disappeared, he wandered seeking her, singing sadly of what he had lost. His songs were so sad that trees shed their leaves when they heard him and a waterfall stopped its motion and turned to ice.

After many months wandering he found himself at the entrance to the Underworld. Since he felt sure he would have found his love if she were still alive he resolved to seek her there. He followed the path downwards till he reached the river. At first the ferryman refused to take him across, saying that the weight of a living man was too much for him to row. But the singer played so lightly and sung so well of the joys of rowing boats that the ferryman took him across with less effort than usual. The singer went on playing, singing lullabies to the fierce hound that guarded the palace until he reached the halls of the Queen of the Underworld.

She asked him why he, a living man, had come to the Underworld, and he replied that he was searching for his love who had disappeared. She said that he must sing for her before she offered any aid. So he sang with all his power, singing of the joy he felt when with his lady, of how much her beauty and spirit had meant to him, and of how sad her loss made him, and as he sang and played the listeners laughed with his joy, cried with his sorrow, and when he stopped playing everyone fell silent. The Queen, Eurydice, spoke: "My justice is wide-ranging, it covers all people. And in justice you do not deserve your love back, for you sung only of what she meant to you and not of what she was to herself. But I can be merciful too. You sing well and perhaps you may learn what you lack if your love returns to you. Go back to the upper world now. Your love will follow behind you. But I warn you not to turn and look at her until you are both back under the light of the sun or you will lose her once more."

Thankfully he turned back. As he went he heard his love's footsteps close behind him. He went ever more lightly and quickly until he came out of the cave entrance and back into the open air. Joyfully he turned to greet her. But he had not thought of where she was, several steps behind him. She was still within the cave. He saw her face and realised that he had been cheated. The steps behind him had not been those of his love; she who had followed him was the Queen Eurydice. He screamed with rage as she went away. He sang so angrily that the ground cracked open around him, and tigers ran away with fear.

He continued to sing with anger for a time, then his songs echoed his loss. As time went on he found himself able to recover some happiness in his songs. In later years he met other women and was happy with them for a time. But always he found in them glimpses of the face of the dark queen Eurydice, and he turned from them in disgust, and so it continued until his death.

"Did his songs last?" you ask. They did not. The singer had some wisdom. He knew that the tapestry of the world is made of many colours, and he could sing many different kinds of songs, as seemed fit on each occasion. But he never learned that the thread from which the tapestry is woven has itself many colours in it, and so each one of his songs contained only one theme. Thus he never recognised his love though she returned to him many times. Each time he rejected her, because he could not accept that she had a dark face as well as a light one. He never learned that Queen Eurydice had not cheated him. For love of him she was willing to return with him to the upper air. She had warned him not to look back until she was in the sunlight and he had not obeyed. He had lost his love because he was only capable of seeing her with her light face and could not recognise her in the aspect she wore in her dark realm.

Many times this singer has been reborn and still he has not learned. At each rebirth of the singer, his songs have lasted for a short while and then faded away. Some day he will be reborn and will have learnt wisdom; when he can see light and dark mixed and not claim the light as better, then his songs will last and inspire us all.

THE LABYRINTH OF THE HEART

DANIEL COHEN

OF POWER, GOOD COUNSEL, AND WISDOM

There was a time when Power and Good Counsel walked hand in hand. That was the springtime of the world. In those days men and women honoured each other and honoured also the living world. The sun, moon and stars, the winds, the waters, and even the rocks themselves were known to be alive. In those days Death was no enemy, but a friend to be welcomed when She made the invitation to visit Her country.

But Good Counsel became pregnant, and Power began to be afraid. He feared first that the coming child would take Good Counsel away from him. And then he feared that their child would so well combine the features of the two of them that it would in due course put him down from his place.

Power devised a plan. He opened his mouth to its widest, and pushed Good Counsel in, swallowing her whole. He now felt free of his fears. He began to claim that all the good counsel in the world now belonged to him, and so he declared that it was only fitting he should rule all the world. Though many opposed his claim, he persuaded, and sometimes bullied, others into believing that this opposition was due to bad counsel. And so, though many grumbled and secretly worshipped elsewhere, he set himself up as ruler of the world.

Though Good Counsel had been swallowed, she remained alive inside Power. Her pregnancy continued, until, unknown to him, she gave birth. The infant found her way in due course to his head, where she emerged fully-grown into the outside world. She was given the name Wisdom. In her struggles to become fully born, she had forgotten her mother's womb, and thought that she was born from her father alone, and that his head was her place of birth. Because of this, she served him devotedly, teaching humans many skills but demanding that these be used only for his benefit. His control over women and men, over the earth and its creatures, grew and grew, until it was so great that it threatened destruction for all.

Then Wisdom began to see that something was wrong. She asked for advice from many people, although she could not tell what they might say that she did not already know. At last she spoke to an old woman, who said "Is it Good Counsel you are looking for?" "Why, yes," Wisdom replied, "I would welcome good counsel from anyone." "Then," said the old woman "I will tell you what I heard from my grandmother, who heard it from hers, and so the tale has passed down many generations. Good Counsel has been missing from the world since your father swallowed her. And she is your mother who you have forgotten."

Wisdom now knew what to do. She approached Power, who was suffering from a stomach-ache from eating too much of the earth's substance. She offered him a drink to heal him of his pains. When he had taken it, he began to vomit up that which had made him ill, until at last Good Counsel, the first being he had swallowed from fear and greed rather than from need, was set free at last.

He looked at her. He looked at his vomit. He saw that what was good and wholesome before he swallowed it had been destroyed because of his greed. He saw that, in being afraid of others, he had made himself lonely; and that through loneliness he had made others into slaves, thinking to force them into love and concern for him. He now realised how much damage he had caused since he swallowed her. Humbly he begged her pardon. She replied that she could only forgive him when he had gone far towards curing the damage he had done.

They both looked at Wisdom, and saw that she combined the best features of both of them. Wisdom looked back, recalling that her parentage did not consist of Power alone, but that Good Counsel too was her parent, and had been missing for much of her life.

Power agreed that he had caused great harm, and that healing the damage was his new task. It was not the work of a day or even of a year. It took many years, even with Good Counsel and Wisdom advising him.

When the task was accomplished, Power discovered that what he had feared and tried to prevent was something to be welcomed. The world was no longer to be ruled by Power, whose dictatorship had led the world close to disaster. Having within her the best of Power and Good Counsel, the new mover and governor of the world was Wisdom.

DANIEL COHEN

ESMERALDA'S QUEST

In the land of the dragons there is one ancient and absolute rule.

Every adult dragon must have a hoard of precious things.

A hoard usually means a lot of things, but that takes many years to gather. The hoards of newly adult dragons are quite small, and are normally made up of the gifts they receive on their two hundredth birthday — the day they become adult.

As Esmeralda was approaching that day, her parents took her to visit other dragons, to help her decide what kind of hoard she wanted.

She saw hoards of gold, plain or worked into necklaces and brooches. "Shiny," she said, "but not what I want."

She saw dragons who collected pearls. "They remind me of the sea, but they are not what I want."

She saw collections of weapons, daggers, swords, axes, some plain, some decorated. "I don't like those at all" she insisted.

She saw precious stones, diamonds, rubies, and emeralds. She was tempted by the emeralds, which reminded her of her own name and colouring, but "Sparkly," she declared "but still not what I want."

"Then what kind of hoard do you want?" asked her parents. "I want one that belongs to me and also to others" was Esmeralda's response.

"Nonsense," said her parents. "There's no such thing", and they took her to see some more.

But Esmeralda remained defiant. "The only hoard I want is one that belongs to me and also to others."

In despair, her parents took her to the Council of Elder Dragons. They thought long, and searched their memories. Finally they declared "Never in the memory of dragonkind has there been a hoard that belonged to one dragon and also to others. Since every adult dragon **must** have a hoard of precious things, Esmeralda is banished from the land of the dragons, and may only return if she can produce such a hoard."

Esmeralda left her home and flew towards the lands of men. It was a long journey and she became hungry. She saw herds of meat animals, and swooped down to take one, just as she would have done at home. With great surprise, she saw men coming out of their houses and shooting arrows at her. She left that place, but wherever she went the same thing happened when she tried to feed. Sometimes men even shot at her as soon as they saw her.

After many days she flew across a forest at the edge of which lived a wise man. He saw her flying, and spoke to her. "You are a beautiful creature. I love the green of your back, and the red edgings to your yellow wings. If only you were smaller, I would love to talk to you and be your friend."

Esmeralda shook herself, and, using some of the magic that all dragons have, she made herself the size of an eagle. Then she shook herself again, and was no larger than a parrot. "Now I can come and stay with you" she said.

She stayed with the wise man for many years. When people visited him, asking for advice, she was there listening. When he told stories to the people she was there listening. When he went to storytelling gatherings, she remained at home. But she got tired of being left by herself. So one day she demanded to go with him to hear stories, and from then on he could be seen at gatherings with a dragon the size of a parrot perched on his shoulder.

She heard about Thomas the Rhymer, how he served the Queen of Elfland for seven years and was rewarded by a tongue that could never lie, she heard how Sir Gawain played the beheading game with the Green Knight, who Sir Gawain married, why he got married and what happened on his marriage. She was reminded of how her ageing great-grandfather fought his last battle, in which he and the human hero Beowulf both perished. She learnt of the young woman who made the difficult journey to the castle East of the Sun and West of the Moon and what happened when she got there, and of another young woman's journey to gain fire from Baba Yaga the powerful. She even learnt the name of the new King of the Cats.

The wise man grew older and frailer. He told Esmeralda to return home when he died. "But what about my hoard" she asked. "I cannot go home without it."

"You will find it when you need it" was his answer.

In time he died. She decided to return home, trusting in what he had said. It was a long journey, and she was still worried about what would happen to her when she got home. To keep herself in good spirits she started to tell herself some of the stories she had learned. She longed to share the stories with her family, and at last understood what he had meant.

"Have you found your hoard?" the Council of Elder Dragons demanded.

"Yes."

"Then where is it?"

"Oh, you can't see it."

DANIEL COHEN

"We have never heard of an invisible hoard," they declared, and began to turn away.

"Listen" said Esmeralda, and began to tell the story of her ancestor and Beowulf. The Council members knew the facts of what had happened, but they had never before heard such a telling. When she had finished, the dragons demanded another story, and she told then of the Firebird and Ivan.

The Council kept demanding more, until she said that she was too tired to continue that night.

They slept, and they dreamed, and the stories wove into their dreams.

When they awoke, the Council of Elder Dragons met together, and discussed Esmeralda.

And they called her before them when she awoke.

"Esmeralda," they said, "Have you more stories?"

"Yes, wise ones, would you like to hear some?"

"We would not only **like** to hear more, we **insist** on it."

She went on telling stories throughout that day.

In the morning, the Council met again, and called her before her.

"It seems," they said "that you have a hoard of stories."

"Yes, wise ones."

"And you will continue to tell stories."

"Of course."

"I loved your stories," said one dragon. "I would like to tell some to my friends. May I do so?"

"Certainly," replied Esmeralda. "These stories do not belong only to me."

And the Council agreed that her hoard of stories was the most precious hoard in all the worlds, and that it belonged to her and to others as well.

DANIEL COHEN

THE INTERPRETER: or An Introduction to Hermeneutics

(**Hermeneutics:** The art or science of interpretation, especially of scripture. *Oxford English Dictionary*)

It was all the interpreter's fault.

He came to our city looking for employment. It was soon clear that he had a wide knowledge of many languages, and most of our merchants began to employ him in their dealings with foreign traders. We saw him speeding from one to another, in those sandals of his with the odd widening at the heels, often pausing to tell one merchant of a recent purchase of interest by another. It seemed that trade prospered with his coming. Our merchants became wealthier and busier than they had ever been. Strangely enough, though, it seemed that the city's thieves also prospered. There were more daring burglaries, more pockets picked on an empty street, than ever before. But this actually added to the city's sense of life, as it all happened without any increase in violence.

His work was so good that we asked him to interpret for several diplomatic missions. Once again we seemed to get the better of the deals, though the foreigners seemed pleased, too. We grew used to seeing him in all parts of the city, using his staff to emphasise points, or bringing it down with a thump when deals were concluded. We admired the spiral decorations running round it — sometimes they seemed to us to be moving, but that was surely no more than a trick of the light.

The trouble arose when we decided that such a cultured man deserved to learn about our religion and the truths it contained.

We showed him one of our sacred scrolls, written in the old language, and we were not a bit surprised when he was able to read and translate it without difficulty.

But then he took the same scroll, and began to read something different from it. "What are you saying?" we asked. "The text does not include this." He answered, "The first time I read, I read the words formed by the ink on the parchment."

We were puzzled; what else was there to read? "But then I read the word still to be formed" he said, "the word waiting patiently to be revealed, to rise out of the white spaces between the letters and to be received". He explained that the original writers had their views on what and who were important enough to be mentioned, as did we present-day readers, and that both we and the writers thereby excluded and oppressed many people. He showed us that every text contains two messages, one formed by the ink and the other by the spaces left between the inked letters, the material included and that which was excluded, and that the message was never complete if only the first text was read.

We asked him to expound to us further. He did so for some time, and then we were surprised to hear him ask "Why were cows so important to your people in the old days?" "But they weren't" we protested, "Cows aren't even mentioned in the sacred books". "That reminds me of the curious incident of the dog in the night-time" was his puzzling reply. "What dog? What night-time?" "Oh, never mind," he said, "I was thinking of an occasion far away in time and space from here".

"But what about the cows," we persisted. "Your people of old included many farmers, and farming is still important to you." "Of course." "And your farms contain horses, sheep, pigs, and cattle, as well as chickens and plants." "Certainly." "Then why do your texts speak of horses, sheep, and pigs, and yet they make no mention of cattle and those who farm them?"

We couldn't answer this. He suggested that this was because cattle, their farmers, their behaviour, and their place in sacred practice, were so well-known to the people in whose times the texts were written that they were taken for granted by the writers, who therefore felt no need to mention them. Yet it was only because of the work of the cattle-farmers that others had leisure to write texts. And so once again he had shown us that what the text does not contain is as important to a true interpretation as what is made explicit in it.

By this time everyone in the city had heard of the new readings he was giving to the old texts. They were being discussed all through the city, at dinner-parties, in public parks, when drinking at an inn; even the comedians were making jokes about him. A passionate interest in theology was now part of people's lives. The priests and the rulers, of whom I am not the least, felt that this would make the city easier to govern. How little we understood!

By now he was talking each week in the main square. One day we noticed an unusually large number of sailors among the crowds. We were surprised, as they had not been greatly involved in the past, but we did not expect that we were seeing the beginning of real trouble. The interpreter began to speak of the sea, and we assumed that the sailors had attended because of some rumour that this might happen.

"The sea is important to you," he said. "Much of your commerce is carried out by sea, there are always ships in the harbour, and many of your people are sailors or involved with shipping." The sailors cheered approvingly. "The sacred texts speak frequently of the sea with great emotion." We all agreed. "And yet, though sailors and the sea are important to you, all the sacred texts were written by landfolk."

DANIEL COHEN

Here we began to be worried, as we heard the sailors start muttering among themselves. We asked how he had determined this. "A wise woman once told me that landfolk are affected differently from sailors by the sea" he began. "She made this clear to me in these words: 'Sailors are surrounded by an unknowable and ever-changing sea that is also a con0000stant in their lives. They cannot carry out their business without it for they live and work on its surface, and yet if they fall into it they cannot survive. Landfolk think they live in a stable place, whereas sailors know that human existence is always precarious and mutable.' "

He stopped at that point, and we all felt we had much to ponder on. We were not surprised to find even more sailors in the crowd the next week. "Why," he began, "since sailors and the sea are so important to you, are sailors not permitted to officiate in temple ceremonies." We explained to him that sailors are always travelling, and cannot be relied upon to be at the temples at the proper times.

"But your merchants travel also in search of new goods and markets, and there is no restriction on them." "That's different," we explained to him at once, "Merchants are settled people, and if one can't be present on some occasion, there is always someone else available for the ceremonies." "Then couldn't the same be done for sailors." Once again we explained to him that the situations were different, but he remained obstinately unable to see any difference.

By that time the sailors were restless. Some of them suddenly unfurled a banner demanding that sailors should have the right to conduct sacrifices on behalf of the people. We hastily declared the day's session closed, and called in the military to persuade people to leave the square quietly.

After that things got worse and worse. Some factions demanded that sailors should have the same religious opportunities that merchants and even farmers had. Others retorted that they could never take part in a ceremony where a sailor officiated; rather than doing so, they would follow another tradition, from which ours had sprung many years ago, that was still resolutely opposed to sailors holding temple office.

Things were in such turmoil that we decided to expel the interpreter whose sayings had so disturbed our peaceful city.

"Why did you do this?" we asked as we pushed him out of the city's main gate.

"If you don't know why change was needed, ask the sailors. Let them write the texts not yet written, let them speak the prophecies not yet spoken. As for myself, where you saw stability I saw sterility. I acted so that you who were high-ranking and powerful would learn that rank and power were not yours by right, and so that you would find the world turned upside down."

"And besides," he added, "I thought it might be an Improoovement."

As he turned and looked at us, we noticed that the swelling on the heels of his sandals were wings, and the spiral decorations round his staff could now be clearly seen to be living snakes coiling and writhing.

"And so," he said with a grin, "I have now given you an introduction to Hermes' New Tricks!"

NEW SHOES FOR NEW WEATHER

Maybe it was just a coincidence. At the time I thought so, but now I doubt it. I was walking along a London street on a rainy day when I saw a brightly lit shop-front in the distance. "Speedy Shoes" it said. I noted without much interest that this was a new shop. Just then I realised that my shoes were leaking badly. Evidently I needed a new pair.

So I squelched along to the shop, and looked at the window. Several pairs looked possible replacements, so I went in. The salesman — perhaps he was the owner, as it was a small shop — approached me. He was a young man with golden hair and a bright smile. I wondered why he was holding a stick, as he didn't seem to have any problems with his legs, but I soon found out that he used it for emphasis, thumping it on the ground just before he said anything he thought was important. And he talked a lot, telling me just why all the pairs I liked weren't right for me. You've heard of people who can talk the hind leg off a donkey. Well, the salesman could have talked that hind leg back onto the donkey.

He was so persuasive that, since he had talked me out of the shoes I liked, I asked him what he would recommend. He brought out an odd-looking pair, which didn't appeal to me at all. "Try them on," he said. "You'll find them so comfortable that you'll think you're walking on air. You'll go so fast that it will feel as if you are flying."

I tried them on, and they did feel comfortable. I still wasn't sure about their appearance, that odd decoration at the front like an eye, and the unusual feathery feel on the outside of the ankles. But, as he continued to praise these shoes as just right for me, I grew inclined to buy them.

"How much are they," I asked. "Fifty-five pounds, ninety-nine pence." I remembered that I had left my chequebook at home, but reached into my wallet for a credit card. They weren't there! I couldn't understand it; I was sure they had been there when I went out, and I hadn't opened my wallet until then. Well, I would just have to check when I got back home.

I pulled out two twenty-pound notes and a ten-pound note from the wallet, and a five-pound note from my pocket. I reached further into the pocket for some change, and found I had ninety pence in my hand. Digging further in revealed only a further seven pence. I was just two pence short. "This will do, won't it," I said, confidently. I was surprised when he answered "No, sir, it won't do. These shoes are a bargain at fifty-five pounds ninety-nine pence. They are worth much more, and I couldn't reduce the price for anyone, not even if he were to thunder at me with all his might."

I began to put my money away, when he made a very strange suggestion. "For you, sir, I will take only fifty-five pounds ninety-seven pence now. But you must promise to pay me the remaining two pence next time you see me. That is, unless you then feel sure that you need the money more for some other purpose." I couldn't understand what he meant. Why was he putting me to so much trouble? And why might I want the money more for some other purpose? And, if I did, why would he let me off the payment?

I put the shoes on — very comfortable they were — and walked out of the store to the nearest station on the London Underground rail system. I was just about to walk down the stairs when I realised that one shoe was very uncomfortable. Sitting down at a bus stop, I took the shoe off. No wonder it was uncomfortable. Though I have no idea how they could have got there, or why I hadn't noticed earlier, I found my credit cards were inside the shoe.

I put them back in my wallet, and had just got the shoe back on when a bus came along. I decided I might as well take it instead of the Underground. A good thing I did so! That was one of the days the whole system was disrupted; if I hadn't stopped when I did, and taken the bus instead, I would have spent two hours stuck in a tunnel.

Well, a couple of days later I went back to the shop. With what the salesman said I felt I had to pay him the tiny amount owing. But the shop was closed, with a notice saying "Closed. Owner gone travelling." I didn't know why he felt we would want to have that extra bit of information.

It's an odd thing about those shoes. Whenever I wear them I find that I end up in the right place. The right place for me, or the right place to help someone, or the right place to get or give some piece of information or news that is needed. And it's not always the place I intended to go to. On one occasion I started out to take my passport to renew it before it expired. But I got sidetracked, and found myself at Heathrow airport. Without quite knowing what I was doing I phoned a friend abroad — not as expensive as it sounds, as I had a calling card with a newly launched telephone company that gave very cheap rates. My friend was in great distress and needed support. I decided to get on a plane for an immediate visit. Yes, those shoes have landed me in some odd places.

No, I haven't seen the salesman again yet, though it's been many years. He seemed certain that I would, and lately I have begun to see why. I haven't been quite so happy wearing the shoes since I realised that. They always take me to the right place to be. Some time that will be near a river-bank, and I'll see him again. He's the one who guides people to the place where one takes the ferry. And, no, I won't give him the two pennies I owe him. I'll have a greater need for them, to pay the ferryman who will take anyone across the river for two pence, but will never take anyone back.

ΕΡΜΗΣ
HERMES
4th c. B.C.

DANIEL COHEN

A SUCCESSFUL EXPERIMENT?

Why are you all looking at me like that? It's not my fault. I only wanted to see what would happen.

You remember how it all started. Baldur had bad dreams — he dreamt of death and Hel's domain. His mother, great Frigga, determined to protect him. She travelled through the nine worlds, demanding a promise from their beings not to harm Baldur. In eight of the worlds she ensured that all beings and all things in that world made this promise.

But in the ninth world, Midgard, the world of men, she acted differently. Why? Was she tired? Did she know what was to happen, and did she permit it?

For in that world she asked all beings and all things on the earth and under the earth, all beings and all things on the sea and in the sea, all beings and all things in the air and above the air, all these she made promise not to harm Baldur.

When she told all this in Asgard, did she look at me — I thought so. She must have known what her actions in the world of men would mean to me.

For I, Loki, am the great trickster and riddle-solver. Lock me in a box, and if there is the slightest hole I will crawl through it. Envelop me in chains, and if there is the least bit of slack I will wriggle free. Sometimes I will create situations of great risk and difficulty just to see how I will find my way out. Even the old oath-breaker, Odin himself, if he wishes to break an oath and keep it at the same time he will come to me for an answer.

So, when Frigga obtained that promise from beings in Midgard she set me a challenge. What was there that was not on the earth nor under the earth, not on the sea nor in the sea, and not in the air nor above the air? Of course I had to see if I could find such a being.

Long did I search. Far did I travel. But all that I saw was on the earth or under the earth, on the sea or in the sea, in the air or above the air. Weary, I came to a house, asked for hospitality, and was granted it. It was Yule, and much merriment was all through the house. I saw a couple embracing under a branch of green with white berries. There are few plants or trees that have berries at this time of year, and I enquired what it was. My host told me it was mistletoe, and took me outside to show me a tree on which it grew.

I looked at it, and then looked again. This mistletoe was not on the earth, for though it grew on a tree yet it was not part of the tree. And it was not in the air, for it was attached to a tree. And most certainly it was not in the earth nor above the air, nor on nor under the sea.

THE LABYRINTH OF THE HEART

My quest seemed to have ended, but I still had to determine if I was right. So I took a branch of mistletoe, formed it into a spear, and gave it and other spears to the blind one, Hodur.

Then I took Hodur to where all you gods were casting stones, trees, and other missiles against Baldur, all of which fell harmlessly. I let Hodur choose a spear and guided him to cast it against Baldur. Like all else it fell without harm. Then Hodur cast another spear. This one hit Baldur and wounded him! No-one could stop the wound bleeding, and Baldur died of the wound.

Why did I give the spears to Hodur the blind, rather than casting them myself? Surely you know that the best experiments are done blind.

I didn't intend Baldur to die. I'm sorry that he's dead. But sometimes experiments have unintended consequences. And I was right, wasn't I? Oh the cleverness of me"

(Later)
"So there you all are again, staring at me. Demanding to know why I disguised myself as a giantess and refused to weep for Baldur.

I disguised myself, of course, so that you wouldn't know it was me, and I wouldn't get into trouble once more.

And I refused to weep because I could see what would happen if I did weep.

Baldur would have returned from Hel's realm, you say. Yes, of course. But what then?

Oh, can't you see? Can none of you gods see further than your own noses? And remarkably ugly noses they are, I must say.

No, not your nose, Iduna. Everyone knows, none better than you yourself, how beautiful you are. And if, by some remote chance, someone did not know, you would soon show them.

And not your nose either, Sif. It's a very pretty nose, as pretty as every other part of you, as I'm sure Thor would agree. What's that, Thor? Are you scowling? Don't scowl, or Sif will think you don't agree with me, and that you don't love her any more.

So, what would have happened if Baldur had returned. Once one had returned from Hel's land, whether god or man, all would be clamouring to be able to return.

They would soon start praying to the returned one, asking for help to rescue them from Hel.

And gradually all prayers would be to Baldur, the returned one, and you gods would no longer be praised. You would decline and dwindle to no more than memories.

I have saved you from that, and now you will punish me.

THE LABYRINTH OF THE HEART

I didn't intend Baldur to die, but I do count it as almost my cleverest trick. What was my cleverest, I hear some of you asking.

Don't you know? Well, I suppose I did take care not to let you know. Creating this wonderful joke of a universe.

DANIEL COHEN

TASTE AND SEE: a midrash on Genesis 3:6 and 3:12

Oh taste, taste and see
How good is the fruit that falls from the tree
Oh taste, taste and see
How good is the fruit of the garden. (Betsy Rose)

Eve was not made from Adam's head to reign over him,
nor from his feet, to be trampled by him,
but from his side, to be his equal,
under his arm, to be protected,
and next to his heart, to be loved. (Traditional)

(**A midrash** originally meant a rabbinic interpretation of a biblical text, but is now used for any creative interpretation of a biblical text that extends and criticises the original.)

Let me tell you how it happened. It's not the way He told Himself it must have happened, the way He persuaded everyone to tell the story. But so far I can still remember the truth, even despite His pressure to tell it His way.

Of course, He blamed Eve.

"You were always the best of My creations," He assured me. "The one most like Me. You always listened to what I said."

"The woman must have tempted you," He decided.

In those days He spoke to me often, and it is true that I listened, perhaps paying too much attention. Then, and later, some of His edicts seemed arbitrary or cruel, but I always assumed He had a good reason for them. Yet somehow He did not bother to talk to Eve.

That led to problems, but it also had advantages for Eve. It made her much freer, more capable of making decisions for herself.

I had named the animals, as He had told me to do. But it was Eve who decided that the plants also needed naming. "Oak," she said, and "rhododendron." Ordinary everyday names, those were, much like animal names such as "cat" and "rhinoceros". But then she got more fanciful. "Forget-me-not", she mused, and "old man's beard".

"I don't understand. What do these names mean?" I asked her.

"They seem the right names somehow. They came to me, and I don't know who suggested them" was all she would answer.

THE LABYRINTH OF THE HEART

And then she came to **that** tree. "Fig," she declared confidently.

I quickly pulled her away from the tree. "You know what He said about that tree," I reminded her.

But she kept going back to that tree, whose smell and appearance delighted her. I could sense her making up her mind.

At last she reached out and touched the fruit. Urgently I called out once more, "You know what He said about that tree".

"He never spoke to me about it. If He wants to ignore me, then I can ignore Him." "I know He told you not to eat. But I don't know if He also wanted me not to eat" she added.

As she plucked the fruit, she said "Good? Evil? I don't know what they mean, but they must mean change of some sort. And we need a change in this unchanging place", as she bit into the ripe fruit.

I knew it would mean trouble, He had warned me often enough, but what was I to do? If she was going to be troubled, then I had to share it. Above even that, I trusted her judgment and admired her courage in choosing change and the unknown rather than staying with what was familiar. So I reached out, took the fruit from her hand, and took a bite myself. And we each ate half of the fruit she had taken.

Well, you know what happened after that. How He asked if we had eaten the fruit He had forbidden. I could have placed the blame on Eve, insisting that it was her fault that I had also eaten the fruit, that she had persuaded me. But I had made the choice to eat it when she offered. If there was a fault, it was mine as much as hers. And so we answered together that we had, that we had felt the need for change. He drove us out of the Garden and pronounced a fate on us.

It's been a hard life since then, with much toil and grief. But there has also been joy.

Eve was right. In the Garden there was no change and so there were no stories. But now there are many stories, and there will be stories until the end of time.

But there is one thing that worries me. He continues to talk to me. And He keeps telling me that I should not have listened to Eve, that I was the head of the household and it was her duty to obey me.

I have always been used to listening to Him, accepting what He says as the truth. So far He has not convinced me when He says this, as I can remember what really happened. But if He keeps on telling me this, sooner or later I will come to believe him. And then the story will take a sadder turn, lasting for many generations, until people stop listening to His voice and seek the truth for themselves.

THE MAN WHO DID NOT LIKE SPIDERS

Once there was a man who did not like spiders.

His father had read him *The Hobbit* and *The Lord of the Rings* when he was a child, and their images of huge spiders catching people in their webs had given him a terror of spiders that remained now he was an adult.

He took particular care to see that there were no cobwebs in his house, he trod on spiders when he saw them on the ground, and he destroyed the webs he saw on bushes. He would not buy bananas, because he had heard that tarantulas had sometimes been found in bunches of bananas. If there was a spider in his bath he turned the water on full and drowned it.

(Do you know, by the way, how to get a spider out of your bath? If you poke at it with a finger or pencil, it will scurry away, but usually will remain at the same level in the bath and not try to climb out. What you do is to take a glass or cup and place it over the spider — make sure the glass is large enough that it does not trap the spider's legs. Then you take a stiff piece of paper and slide it under the glass. The spider will then be on top of the paper and under the glass. You can lift it all up and let the spider loose where you see fit — perhaps outside, perhaps on a ledge in the bathroom.)

One day he was walking in a garden admiring the roses. Seeing a spider's web attached to a rose bush, he angrily tore it apart, not caring if there was a spider there or not. The spider jumped from the web and bit him. At first he thought it was nothing, but gradually he found himself walking slower and slower until he was unable to walk at all. As he stood there, spiders came up and began to weave their silk around him, until he was cocooned with no possibility of escape.

He remained like this for many days, at first in anger and then in self-pity. It seemed to him that there were voices in his ear, but as they were spiders' voices he refused to listen. At last, feeling abandoned by everyone, he started to listen to the voices.

He found that the spiders were telling him about themselves. They began by speaking of the connections between spiders and humans. They told him of a famous spider of many years ago. She was attempting to spin a web in a cave. Time after time one of her threads came unstuck and she had to begin all over again. It was only on the seventh time that she succeeded. She became famous among humans because a man who was hiding from his enemies after losing many battles was watching her. That man was Robert the Bruce; she inspired him to fight one more time, and he won independence for Scotland.

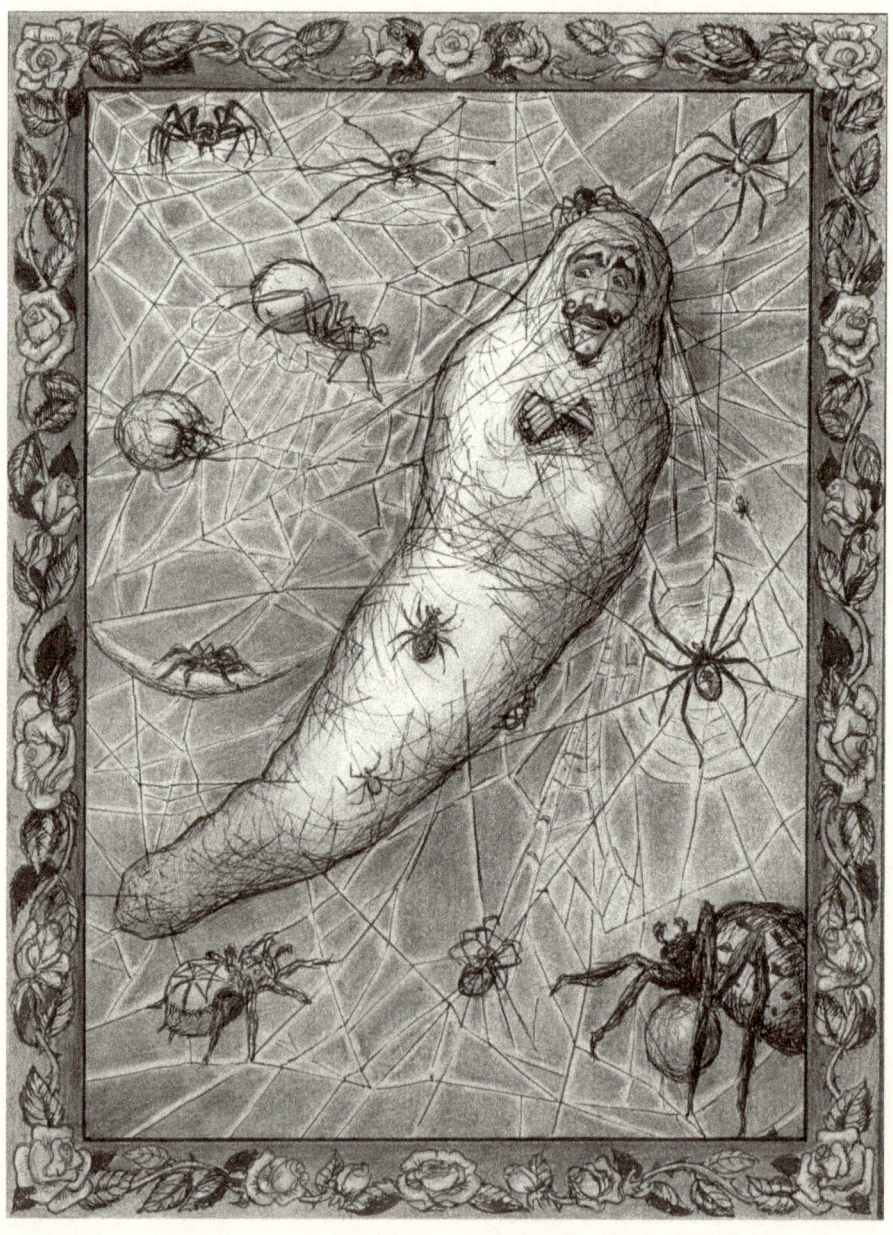

They told also of the spider who saved a great man (some say it was the prophet Mohammed) from his enemies. He too hid in a cave. The searchers thought no-one could have gone inside because an unbroken spider-web crossed the mouth of the cave. The spiders praised their heroic ancestress who, seeing him enter, had exhausted herself by spinning her large web before the arrival of the searchers.

They told him of Dr. Thomas Muffet, that ardent admirer of spiders, who in the sixteenth century wrote the book *Theatrum Insectorum* with much information about spiders. They sounded, though, a little annoyed at being called insects, and showed him all their eight legs, two more than any mere insect.

They went on to speak of Dr. Muffet's daughter Patience. Patience Muffet, they insisted, was not frightened away when a big spider sat down beside her. She simply left her tuffet to call her father to look at an unusual spider.

They reminded him of the old rhyme — which he claimed never to have heard —

If you wish to live and thrive
Let a spider run alive.

The man who disliked spiders attempted to move, but he was still paralysed. The numbness was beginning to wear off, however, and he felt pain stronger than he had ever felt before.

They went on to speak of the days when spiders were signs of the Goddess. It was lucky to have a spider run over you, since that was a message from the Goddess. Though we no longer remember why it is lucky, we still declare that it is good luck to have a money spider run over us.

They spoke of Arachne, the Greek Goddess who wove on her web all the tales of the younger gods and goddesses. Her tale was distorted in later times; it was said that she was a woman turned into a spider because she claimed she could spin and weave better than the goddess Athene. To this day her name is commemorated in the scientific name *arachnids* for spiders and their relatives.

The spiders continued to speak, and, to his surprise, he found he liked listening to them. He still felt pain, but there were now flashes of joy.

They made mention of Anansi, that great trickster spider man, who travelled with his people from Ghana to the West Indies.

The spiders spoke too of the Native American's reverence for Spider Woman or Grandmother Spider. There are some who say that when all the world was without light, Grandmother Spider was the one who flew up to the sun, and gathered a small spark of it to benefit humans. Others say that Spider Woman was the first being formed by the Creator Spirit, and that it was her task to create life in the world — she was told that through her knowledge, wisdom, and above all else her love she would bless all created beings.

Yet others say that it was Grandmother Spider who, when one world suffered destruction, helped us to reach the next world. That world was destroyed because humans forgot that they were not separate one from another. Now, in this world which is named the Upper World we are connected to her by the threads she spun, and connected to other beings through our links with her. She warned us that to survive and to learn to be true humans we must remember this and always keep it in mind.

These tales, and many more, they told to the man as he remained cocooned. Their stories cured him of the terror of them that he had felt for so long. He kept endeavouring to move, and found that he was now able to make small movements of his limbs, which slowly became more definite. The sense of pain and of joy intermingled seemed to go deeper and deeper into his heart.

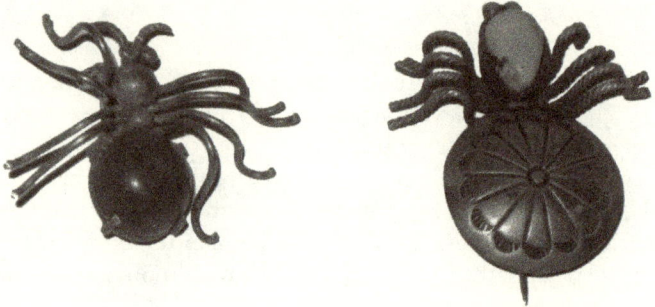

They began to speak of their own lives, telling him first of the great number and variety of spiders that can be found in England, where he lived. They were proud that there were nearly six hundred different species of spiders in England. Some live on mountain-tops, others in greenhouses; some like to be near water, some can live without it; some hunt in the daytime, others at night. They made him realise how much humans would be plagued by insects if it were not for spiders. They told him that the weight of the insects they consumed in a year in England exceeded the total weight of the humans who lived there. Even in the garden he had been walking in, though it was not large, there were many hundreds of thousands of spiders, only a few of which had revealed themselves to him.

They showed him their eight eyes, both large and small; for those spiders who hunt rather than making webs, the small upward-facing eyes respond to movement, the ones at the side help in judging distance, and the large central ones magnify the prey.

They pointed out that not all spiders spin webs. There are those that hunt and others whose home is in a tube of silk, in which they hide till an insect touches it, when they reach through the silk to pull it in. There are those who live under water and breathe by trapping bubbles of air in their silk balloons. None of these make webs. Even among those who spin webs there are many types. Some live in their webs, others remain nearby and only enter their webs when the trembling of its threads show that there is an insect caught. All these and more they showed him, among them the little red spider (which is not a spider at all, but a mite, though these are not far distant from spiders). He saw pink spiders, grey ones, brown ones, and even one which was mostly black with touches of scarlet. He saw tiny spiders, less than one-tenth of an inch in length, and larger ones of more than five inches.

At last he appreciated the wonders of the creatures he had disliked for so long. The silk in which he had been enclosed began to dry and split, until at last it was only tatters about him. Tentatively he put out his foot, and began walking. As he walked out of the garden, he noticed a spider's web on a rose bush. Drops of rain resting on it reflected the sun, and the brilliant display seemed to him a vision of heaven.

Once there was a man who liked spiders.

DANIEL COHEN

THE MATHEMATICIAN WHO HAD LITTLE WISDOM

Once there was a mathematician who had little wisdom. One spring he attended a conference in Scotland on group theory, which was his research speciality. Since the conference was long, he decided to take a couple of days off, which was certainly wise. He had heard much about the beauty of Scotland's rivers, and the fine salmon that swam in them, so he decided to go salmon-fishing. He did not think of the need for a licence, nor that a large charge is made for the right to fish for salmon in most places; indeed, he had not even checked whether there were salmon in the rivers at that time of year. This may seem foolish of him, but turned out not to be so.

He went to the River Tweed, which was running sweetly. He saw many people fishing for salmon, but found a pool where no-one was. Not thinking that this might be because that was not a good place for salmon (for he had little wisdom, though, as we shall see, he was also lucky), he began fishing under a bright spring sky. And, after he had been fishing for some time, his good luck hooked a fine salmon, and, after a struggle, he landed it. Great was his surprise when the salmon spoke to him. "Put me back," it said, "put me back in the river before I die."

The mathematician had little wisdom but he was just wise enough to do as the salmon asked. I have heard some suggest that he should have kept the salmon in a tank, and make much money by exhibiting it as a talking fish. Even on the everyday level, this idea is foolish, since he had no way to compel the salmon to talk. But there are deeper reasons why this thought was foolish. It may well be that we are on the brink of disaster because we treat the world as something to be exploited for financial profit, rather than as something sacred. Be that as it may, to treat the creatures of the inner worlds in such a way is a certain recipe for disaster.

The salmon, now returned to the river, spoke again. "I am the Salmon of Wisdom. I have fed on the Nuts of Knowledge that fall from the hazel tree which leans over the Well at the World's End. Since you have set me free, I will grant you a gift."

Now the mathematician had been thinking hard about a problem in his special area of research, which is known as group theory. "I have been looking at a particular group," he said, "and I would like to know which of its members have a certain property that interests me. I would like to have a machine which would tell me, when I give it a member of that group, whether or not it has that property."

THE LABYRINTH OF THE HEART

The salmon replied, "I must warn you that if you ask me for something impossible I will vanish, and what little wisdom you have may become even less." "That's no problem," answered the mathematician. "I know that there are some groups for which no such machine exists, but I have shown that in this case it can be done."

So the salmon swam deeper into the river, and returned carrying a little machine. It looked very delicate and attractive, and the mathematician was delighted by it. He took it home, and used it with great pleasure for several weeks. He enjoyed looking at it, for it was indeed a work of art, and his eyes kept following the tracery of lights that showed the machine was operating, finishing with either a green light or a red one. Since this machine was not of the ordinary world, it never ran out of memory in which to perform the computation.

But after a while the mathematician, who had little wisdom, became dissatisfied, and decided to ask the salmon for a more powerful machine. He went back, with the machine, to the pool where he had first caught the salmon. The river was running high, and the skies were grey, but he did not notice that. "Salmon," he called, "Great Salmon of Wisdom, I desire a gift from you".

The salmon came up to the surface and spoke. "What is it this time?"

"This machine is very nice, but I would like a machine that does more. I don't just want a 'yes' or 'no' answer to my question each time. When the answer is 'yes', I would like to know exactly why that is."

"Remember, if you ask for the impossible, I will vanish and you may lose even what little wisdom you have."

"I feel quite sure that, since you have given me one machine, you can also give me the more powerful one I desire."

"You are right," said the salmon, and swam deeper into the river. He emerged carrying a heavy and ugly machine. The mathematician dragged it home. For several weeks he was happy using it.

But after a while, since he had little wisdom, he became dissatisfied, and decided to ask the salmon for a more powerful machine. With an effort, he dragged the machine back to the pool where he had first seen the salmon. It was a hard journey, under a black sky, with thunder in the distance, and showers of hail. When he arrived, the river was in flood, and lapped almost to his feet. Since he had little wisdom, he did not see what this had to do with him, and once more called out, "Salmon, Great Salmon of Wisdom, I desire a gift from you."

The salmon came up, and asked what he wanted this time. "This machine does what I asked for, but it is so slow. There have been many occasions when a word for which the first machine answered my question in a few seconds, has taken days on this new one. What I want now is a machine which will do what the second machine does, but will do it as fast as the first machine."

"I'm getting tired of your demands," said the salmon crossly. "Is that what you really want?" The mathematician, who had little wisdom, did not notice the warning in the salmon's tone, and said, firmly, "Yes, that's what I want."

At that, the salmon leapt into air, cried out "What you ask is impossible!", and fell back into the river with a splash that drenched the mathematician. When he recovered from being soaked, the salmon and the machine were gone.

As he began to start homewards, the salmon appeared briefly, and said, "Read computer science journals, as well as mathematics journals. Then, it may be that instead of losing what little wisdom you have, you may even gain some."

When the mathematician returned to his home university, he did as the salmon had suggested, and started to look at computer science journals, including back issues. He learned why his last request was impossible. The group he was looking at was closely connected with a particular computer program. It turned out that his two questions could be solved by solving similar questions about this program. And computer scientists had long ago discovered that one of those questions had an easy answer, while the other one was hard.

The last I heard of him, he was still looking at these journals, and also at journals in mathematical logic, as well as those more directly concerned with his own interests. He discovered, to his surprise, that, though superficially far distant from his own area of research, they contained a significant number of results important to him. By reading them, his wisdom had increased.

DANIEL COHEN

THE BALLAD OF JACK GREEN
(for Alan Acacia, a wise April fool)

Jack Green woke up on the first of May.
Said "It's time to dance to my work today."

So Jack went dancing down the street.
With "I wish you joy" all the folk he'ld greet.

Then Jack danced on for a couple of miles.
Behind him the frowns were turned to smiles.

The doors of his office flew open wide
As Jack danced in, with a skip and a slide.

Jack sat down at his desk to phone,
But his feet kept tapping a beat of their own.

His feet kept dancing a rhythm so sweet
That he danced from his office and into the street.

Behind him followed both typist and clerk,
Into the sunlight, away from their work.

From office and shop danced women and men,
Glad to be out in the open again.

Down the streets of the city they all followed Jack,
Through the town hall and then they danced back.

Wherever they danced grew bushes and flowers,
Till covered with leaves were the grim city towers.

The people watched Jack dance far away.
— "In another city you'll find me next May."

THE LABYRINTH OF THE HEART

DANIEL COHEN

THREE WORLDS, TWO QUEENS, ONE PRINCE

Young Headstrong was our nickname for him in Dyfed, our prince, Pwyll. Act first, think later, that was always his way. Strange in someone whose very name means 'thought'; perhaps he wanted to show that he was not bound by his name, or, more likely, his parents knew what his nature would be and hoped his name would change that behaviour.

I remember the day it all started, when we out hunting. A great stag crossed our path, and Pwyll raced after it, crying "That's **my** stag", ignoring the bellowing of hounds from nearby.

He soon outdistanced us. When he found us again, he seemed changed. More mature, more serious. His judgements and his rule were better than they had been, more thoughtful. It wasn't until a year later that we learnt why. He called us together one day, and asked how his rule of the land had been. "Better than ever" we said, and he told us why this was, reminding us of the day he had gone after that great stag.

After a long chase he and his hounds caught up with the stag in a clearing, just after the hounds that he had heard also reached the stag. Angrily he beat them. Not a good thing to do! It surprised us that even Young Headstrong would be so bold as to offend the master of white hounds with red ears. Still, good came of it.

Soon their master appeared, and berated Pwyll for his discourtesy. Pwyll, thinking at last (he often managed to think after acting, but sometimes it was too late) apologised for his discourtesy and asked who the stranger was and what he demanded in recompense.

"I am Arawn" was the reply, and Young Headstrong knew that he had offended a king of the Otherworld. "You must enter my land of Annwn, stay for a year and a day, and then do me a service." "Gladly will I do this," replied Pwyll, "but what will become of Dyfed in my absence." "I shall put on your shape, as you will put on mine, and I will rule Dyfed for you. None shall know that the lands do not have their own rulers; and you must ensure that none shall know of it" came the response. "And no harm to come to Dyfed!" (I told you that Pwyll was capable of thought). "None. Indeed, only good." "Then it is settled."

And so we learned that last year we had been ruled by Arawn, and well-ruled we had been.

Meanwhile, Pwyll had been ruling in Annwn, and at the end of that year and a day had set out, as Arawn desired, to fight with Hafgan, who ruled a neighbouring kingdom. Arawn himself had fought the previous year, a fight that had ended in equality, and only a man of Earth could win the battle for him. Pwyll walked through woods of oak and alder to meadows by a river, and walked down to the ford. Hafgan approached from the other side, and they fought in the water, the neutral territory.

Blows were exchanged, sword hitting sword or shield, no blood being let, until both were tiring. Then Pwyll brought his sword down in a mighty blow that cut off Hafgan's sword-arm. "I shall die of this blow" cried Hafgan, dropping his shield. "Be courteous and strike off my head, that at least my death will be speedy." Young Headstrong raised his sword for a blow at the neck, but then he remembered Arawn's advice (action had nearly overcome thought) and dropped it. For he had been warned that one stroke would kill, but a second one would heal again.

Now that Pwyll had won the battle for Arawn, the two returned to their proper places.

"Tell us of Arawn's court" we all asked, and Pwyll recounted its many splendours. "What of the women" our young men asked, and "What of the women" asked our young women. "Beautiful they were, and wise, but the finest was Arawn's queen. Hair black as midnight, skin as fair as the full moon, eyes as full of lights as the stars in the sky, and power and wisdom to match her beauty."

"Your nights must have been a delight" I, and the other young men, joked, with a touch of envy. "No, indeed, they were full of pain and torment, and it may have been my frustration that spoke through the blow that killed Hafgan." "How so. Surely she would not deny her body to the lord she loved." "No, indeed" said Pwyll, "but I was not that lord, though she thought so. Difficult it was not to make love to such a lady, and she most willing. Had I been Arawn in truth, or if she had known me for Pwyll, and still wished for love, then indeed I would have made love most willingly, and all would have been joy. But I was another in Arawn's guise, and she did not know it. So in all honour and courtesy, though it saddened her since she did not know the cause, I could only refrain."

Now Pwyll's advisers decided it was time he got married, for the land needed a woman to rule it also, and they suggested many possible brides for him. But he rejected them all; one was too short, another too tall; one was too serious, another too frivolous; one too young, another too old. At last, his senior adviser burst out, "It will be a wonder if our prince ever finds a woman to suit him."

"A wonder, is it" cried Young Headstrong. "Then I will climb the Hill of Arberth and see what comes of it." For the power of that hill was that whoever should spend a night there would either receive many blows and buffets or would see a wonder. You can be sure all the young men had tried it, and all had been driven down by blows; we began to think that only one of the royal line would get to see a wonder.

THE LABYRINTH OF THE HEART

So next night Pwyll climbed the hill, while his war-band stood at the foot. At midnight he saw a woman riding slowly along the road on a white horse. He called to the fastest runner among us, to overtake her and find out who she was and what she wanted. It should have been easy to catch such a slowly walking horse, but no matter how fast he ran her horse was always some distance ahead.

The following night Pwyll climbed the hill again, while we remained below. Once more the woman appeared, her horse walking slowly. He called on me to ride after her, as I had the best horse of all his followers. I trotted. It should have been easy to catch up with her, but she was always the same distance ahead of me. I galloped, but it made no difference. I lashed my horse to greater effort, which is not my custom, but she was still that distance ahead. I let my exhausted horse stop. She looked back at me, and I saw that she had hair black as midnight, skin as fair as the full moon, and power and wisdom to match her beauty, and angry eyes full of lights as the stars in the sky. She looked down at my horse, and I thought I heard her say "Poor horse." You can be sure that when we returned home, I gave my horse the best care and the best food that he had ever had.

On the third night, it all began as before. This time, Pwyll followed her on his own horse. He soon saw that even galloping would not catch her, and (thinking at last, as he usually did given time) he halted his horse and called out to her. She stopped, and they began talking.

He returned to us with a broad grin, and said "She came here for love of me, and has agreed to be my wife. But I nearly lost her. If I had continued to chase after her, and had not stopped and asked her to stop and talk, she would not have returned." "But who is she?" "She is Rhiannon, daughter of a king whose land is both far from here and near. But we cannot get married for a year and a day"

At the end of the year, we set out, in our best attire. We rode by hilly ways and hollow ways, through forests, fording broad rivers and crossing deep rivers by bridges so narrow that our horses had difficulty keeping their footing. It was only a short time before we realised that we were in lands we had never seen before. At length we entered a cavern in a hillside. It was glowing with precious stones, and strange formations of stone rose from the floor and dangled from the roof. Leaving the cavern, we saw broad meadows a little below us, with tables laid out for a feast, and a great king seated at the head of one table, Rhiannon at his right side, and a handsome glowering man at his left. Pwyll was greeted, and seated next to Rhiannon, and we all began to feast, to listen to the bards, and to converse.

Then the glowerer arose, and said "It is an auspicious day." "It is indeed" said Pwyll. "On such a day" continued the glowerer "boons should be granted." "Indeed they should," replied Young Headstrong, ignoring the elbowing Rhiannon was giving him. "Ask what you want, and if it is in my power, you shall have it." "Then give up your claim to Rhiannon. She was promised to me many years ago." It would be the worst of fates to go back on one's word, especially in such a place. And so we left despondently, though Rhiannon talked urgently to Pwyll before we left.

At the end of a further year, Pwyll called us to set out once more, this time walking and dressed in rags. We walked by hilly ways and hollow ways, through forests, fording broad rivers and crossing deep rivers by bridges so narrow that we had difficulty keeping our footing. It was only a short time before we realised that we were in lands we had seen only oncebefore. At length we entered a cavern in a hillside. It was glowing with precious stones, and strange formations of stone rose from the floor and dangled from the roof. Leaving the cavern, we saw broad meadows a little below us, with tables laid out for a feast, and a great king seated at the head of one table, Rhiannon at his right side, and to her right that handsome man, not glowering this time. We, seeming beggars as we were, with sticks and crutches, stood far apart from the wedding party.

At the height of the festivities, Pwyll approached and said "It is an auspicious day." "It is indeed;" came the reply. "On such a day boons should be granted." "Indeed they should. Ask what you want, and if it is not excessive, you shall have it." Pwyll produced a bag from under his cloak, and said "Food for me and my friends. Enough to fill this bag is all I request." "Granted."

And so food was put into the bag. Food from one table, but the bottom of the bag was only just covered. Food from more tables was put in, until there was no more food left, but still the bag was only half-full. "Can this bag ever be filled?" "It can, but only if one who is true lord over all he claims as his shall step into the bag and say 'Bag, be full'."

Then the handsome man stepped into the bag, and said "Bag, be full." But he was not true lord over all he claimed as his, for, instead of filling, the bag instantly rose to cover him.

Pwyll quickly tied it up., and took his stick and knocked the bag to me. My stick rose to knock the bag to another of us. And soon the bag was being knocked from one of us to another. Many sporting contests with ball and stick have their origin in that day.

A voice came from the bag "Is there no end to this beating?" "There is, if you give up your false claim to Rhiannon, who wishes to marry me." "Granted." "And no harm to me and mine from you and yours" said Pwyll, thinking once more. "Granted."

Another year and a day passed, and this time nothing marred the wedding of Pwyll and Rhiannon. I was delighted to be made captain of the Queen's guard. Even my dear wife was not too angry with me when I said "Rosie, my love, you are the second most beautiful woman in the world."

But the land needed an heir. At the end of the first year, there was no sign of a child. The same at the end of the second year. When there was still no child at the end of the third year, people began to mutter that no child could come from one from the Unchancy Lands. You can be sure that the muttering stopped when I was around, but I could not be everywhere.

Pwyll himself stopped the muttering in the best way possible. At last Rhiannon was with child. Great was the joy in the land, and greater when the birth of a son was announced. But the joy quickly turned to despair as the horrible news came from the midwives. Headstrong (no longer Young Headstrong) made the rashest action of his life. How could he have believed the evil that the midwives spoke? How could he not have trusted his own true queen?

Even now, years later, when all has turned out well, I can hardly bear to recall that day. My mouth is dry, my tongue is thick in my throat. I cannot speak of it. Let others tell the rest of the tale.

You can read in the Mabinogion how Rhiannon fell asleep, exhausted by the birth, with the baby between her and the wall. Her attendants fell into a deep sleep, and awoke to find the child had disappeared. Terrified that they would be blamed for not watching, they smeared blood on Rhiannon's lips and hands, and claimed she had killed and eaten the child. This was believed, since she was not of human race, and she was severely punished. The nature of the punishment, what had happened to the child, and how they were re-united, can also be found in the Mabinogion.

DANIEL COHEN

THE SEER IN THE HAWTHORN TREE

"I re — mem — ber." The words came slowly and creakily, the voice sounding like a hinge that had not been used for a long time and needed oiling. "I remember." More confident now, but still sounding stiff through lack of use.

The sound seemed to be coming from near the ancient hawthorn tree with the crack in its trunk, but no-one was visible. Then the crack widened, and a man stepped out from within the tree. His head brushed the branches, and white blossoms settled on his hair.

"I remember," he said for a third time. He looked at the flat expanse of green, with the brown and the white blobs standing up from it. "Cows — and sheep — in a field," he said, dredging the words up from a great depth. He looked over to where, through some trees, he heard a gurgling sound, and saw light flashing. "Sunlight on a stream," he thought, remembering that this had always been his favourite landscape.

He walked towards the stream, and crossed it. His feet knew where the stepping-stones were. In the distance, across several fields, he could see a bonfire and people dancing round it. He went towards them.

As he walked, he remembered more and more. He knew who he was, though as yet he did not know why he was here nor what had happened to him. He was the Seer, the advisor of the Protector. His visions and magic had always helped those who defended the land of Britain against invaders.

But who had the defenders been, and who the invaders? Had he been helping the Roman inhabitants and the Tribes, some in Roman togas and others fiercely refusing Roman ways, against the Saxons? Or were the Romans the invaders, and the Tribes, painted in woad, the defenders? Or, even earlier, were the Tribes the invaders, and the small dark-haired people the defenders?

In all these struggles he had been present. Throughout the years invaders had come, as had those seeking refuge, and some had settled in the land. In due course they found their place, the land accepted them, and they became defenders against a new invasion.

A few words drifted to him from the people chanting around the bonfire. "Nimue … come to us."

Of course, Nimue. She who had played such a great part in his life. But was she the young woman to whom he had taught magic and the arts of the seer, or was she the old woman who had taught him those arts?

It was Nimue who had sealed him inside the hawthorn tree, he remembered that. Why? It was not so that she would be the greatest magician and seer, of that he was certain. And, though she loved him, it was not to keep him to herself that she had imprisoned him. He was sure

THE LABYRINTH OF THE HEART

that men would believe these were the reasons, but they were not, though he could not yet recollect why she had done so.

Slowly the memory came back to him. He had been tired, so tired, after his work through the centuries. She had promised him rest, and the time to regain his strength and powers. She had placed him inside her tree to protect him, and told him that the time would come when he would emerge refreshed, needed once more.

As the memories rushed back, he formed verses from them and declaimed them.

> In the region of the summer stars
> The journeyer rests awhile.
> The wheel turns, as it always does.
> Returning to earth, he takes form again.
> Salmon, dove, hare, grain.
> Otter, hawk, hound, hen pursue.
> The child is born, the wind is fresh.
> The young lad smells the nearby cows.
> The youth joins in the songs
> And dances to the fiddle and drum.
> The man hears stories told.
> He tells them again, changed yet the same.
> With tales of many lands his head is full.
> The young woman listens with joy to the stories.
> He is tired. She opens the crack in the hawthorn tree.
> He enters. She closes the crack and he rests.
> When the tree opens again he emerges.
> Is play his wisdom or is wisdom his play?

A curl of smoke from the bonfire reached him. He smelled apple wood and hazel, oak and holly, hawthorn and blackthorn, ash and rowan and yew. A fire of nine trees. Those who had lit the fire must have a great purpose in mind.

He continued towards them. They had called on Nimue — had they known of his presence, and was it their actions that had awakened him? Certainly it had been time for him to wake. In the old days the inhabitants of the land has defended it against invaders. But now, he sensed, they were themselves destroying the land. They thought that they owned the land, that it was theirs to do what they wished with. They had forgotten that they belonged to the land, not the land to them.

He looked at the huge fields nearby, all yellow with a crop he did not recognise. Stretching out his mind, he learned that it was called rape — a fitting name, he thought. There were no hedgerows, no food for the small creatures, no places for the birds to nest. The old inhabitants of the land, the small beings of this world and the beings of the Otherworld, were being driven out in the name of profit.

There were those who tried to recall the old ways, naming themselves pagans or Druids, and others who also understood the needs of the land. But they too had been corrupted by the prevailing ideas. They held their rites in groves and stone circles, even at the great Giants' Dance on Salisbury Plain. But it was only rarely that they remembered to ask the dwellers and guardians of those groves and circles for permission to work there, and even rarer for them to ask those beings what they desired.

All his powers were going to be needed. He could see what must be, what it was too late to change. He could see what might be, for good or bad. This was a struggle even greater than those of the old days.

Now he was nearly at the bonfire. He remained in the shadows, listening to their chant.

> Nimue, Dark One, Lady of magic and enchantment,
> From your home in the Forest of Broceliande, come to us.
> Nimue, Light One, Lady of hawthorn and all blossoming trees,
> From your home in the Forest of Broceliande, come to us.
> Nimue, chooser of all prophets and seers,
> From your home in the Forest of Broceliande, come to us.
> Nimue, lover of all prophets and seers,
> From your home in the Forest of Broceliande, come to us.
>
> Nimue, who inspired the Wise One, be with us.
> Nimue, who let him rest in his old age, be with us.
> Nimue, who opened your hawthorn tree for him to sleep inside, be with us.
> Merlin's Enclosure, the Isle of Britain, calls out to you.
> He has been asleep twice seven hundred years.
> Nimue, open up your hawthorn tree once more.
> Nimue, let him awake and emerge rejuvenated.
> Nimue, kind one, grant us a seer.
> Nimue, unrelenting one, give us inspiration.

Finally, he stepped into their circle. "You called. I awoke. I am Merlin."

DANIEL COHEN

PITY THE POOR EMIGRANT

Down by the salley gardens my love and I did meet,
She passed the salley gardens on little snow-white feet.
She bade me take love easy, as leaves grow on the tree,
But I was young and foolish, with her did not agree.

It was a poor town, ours. The one rich man in it had given us a park, with an avenue of willows by the river. My love used to meet me there after work. She would dance up to me, kiss me, and run away, daring me to follow. But I would call on her to be serious, that we had to work out how we could afford to get married.

At last I realised that our only chance was for me to go overseas, to a land of opportunity where I could earn enough money for us. Before going, I wove a little box out of willow twigs, and tied a ribbon to it to make a pendant for her neck. I would have liked to place a ruby or diamond in it, to show off her lovely skin. But all I had to put in it for her was my heart, which she said was more than any rubies or diamonds to her.

Before boarding the ship that would separate us, I told her that in a year, or two, or five at the most, I would have enough money to send for her, and we could get married. She promised to wait for me while the sun shone at noon. While I was waiting for the ship to leave, I twisted a long thin willow branch into a circle, and placed it as a band on my hat.

All around my hat I shall wear the green willow,
All around my hat for a twelvemonth and a day,
And if anyone should ask me why it is I wear it,
I wear it for my true love who is far far away.

And so, arrived in that foreign country, I travelled to a place where some of my own townsfolk had settled, and soon got good work. After a year I wrote to my love saying that I was prospering, and that in a year, or two, or four at the most, I would have enough money to send for her, and we could get married. She wrote back that she would wait for me for as long as the night sky held stars.

In the second year I set up on my own making my new inventions that everyone wanted. At the end of that year I wrote to my love to say that in a year, or two, or three at the most, I would have enough money to send for her and we could get married. She wrote back that she was waiting for me to send for her, but that the waiting was cruelly hard.

During the next three years I began to make my fortune. My factories were working hard, and their smoke dimmed the sun at noon; at night the smoke covered the sky so that no stars could be seen.

THE LABYRINTH OF THE HEART

At the end of that time I wrote to my love that now I had the money for us to get married, and that I could give her the diamonds and rubies that she deserved as adornment. She wrote back that joy that was near was better than far-away joy, and that she had now married a young man back home.

The willow tree it will twist
And the willow tree it will twine.
Would that I were in that young girl's arms
That once had been a true love of mine.

With more and more factories, over the years I became a rich man. I gave the people of the town a park, with an avenue of willows by the river. Young men and women would meet there when their work was ended. The willows were gold in the spring with catkins, a gold fairer than the gold of the coins I now had. But the gold of the catkins was not so fair as the golden hair of my lost love.

In a field by the river my love and I did stand,
And on my leaning shoulder she placed her snow-white hand.
She bade me take life easy, as grass grows on the weirs,
But I was young and foolish, and now am full of tears.

JOHNNY FAA'S INDICTMENT

We are seven brothers of a song
We all are wondrous bonnie-O,
And this very night we all shall be hanged
For stealin' of the Earl's lady-O.

They will hang us tonight, my brothers and me. The trial is today, but the verdict is certain. What else but foul sorcery could bring an earl's lady to run away with a gypsy?

The gypsies came to our good lord's gate
And O but they sang bonnie!
They sang so sweet and so complete
That down came our fair lady.

She came tripping down the stair
And all her maids before her;
As soon as they saw her well-faured face
They cast their glamourie o'er her.

He was a poet, that earl. And a fine poet too, I must admit. He wrote poems to his lady wife that were admired by those who heard them. But he did not understand the effect those poems had on her, he did not know that poems could be magic. His poems told her exactly who she was, what she thought and felt, and how she behaved; they gave his understanding of her and not her own. He bound her in his cool web of language like a spider's prey, and like a spider he sucked the juices from her. His songs were so sweet and so complete that they cast a spell on her that charmed the heart from her, till her life was his and not her own.

And then we came. The travelling people, never content in one place, but always desiring change. We came with our ribbons and mirrors for sale and spices from distant lands, with our juggling and fire-eating. The common folk of the castle clustered round us, and we began to sing.

The Earl's wife moved down the stairs to listen to us. My heart was caught as I saw her, and I made new songs for her. She came closer, and my songs asked her questions. "Who are you, my lady, do you know who you are?" "Here is a dance, lady will you join in it?" "I have a heart to give away, lady will you take it?"

They've gi'en tae her the nutmeg fine,
They've gi'en tae her the ginger-O.
She's gi'en tae them a far better thing,
The gowd ring frae off her finger-O.

The questions seemed to free her, she laughed and looked lovelier than ever. She took the gold wedding ring from her finger and tossed it to me. I spun it round three times, tossed it into the air and it disappeared in mid-flight.

And she pulled off her high-heeled boots,
Made of Spanish leather O.
"Last night I slept with my own wedded lord,
And tonight with the gypsy laddie O."

And so we rode away, my brothers and I, and she rode with us. I took delight in showing her the land as it truly was, close to and not from a distance. I showed her how to catch trout, putting a hand quietly into the stream under a fish where it lay resting, and moving her fingers rhythmically closer and closer to the trout; then closing the hand quickly and flipping the fish onto land. She was soon more supple at this than I, and I had always been reckoned the best.

The first time she startled a hare and it ran straight into one of the snares she had made from her own braided hair and a few twigs and branches, she laughed with delight. Then she cried as I picked up the dead animal, and she realised that she was responsible for its death. And she laughed again when she tasted the stew I made from that hare, and the wild garlic and the sorrel that I picked. And always she both laughed and cried as her snares caught beasts and birds for food, laughing that she was so skilful, crying that creatures had to die to feed us.

She lay in my arms in the moonlight, and we gazed at the mass of glittering stars. I saw the best of dark and light in her face and eyes, and knew the mystery of cloudless starry nights was echoed in her power and beauty.

I sang at the fairs, and I admit that I was surprised when her strong voice made a harmony with my own. But I was even more surprised and delighted when she started songs herself, and I realised that they were not ones she had learned but were entirely her own.

We moved through the summer and into autumn. I showed her the crops ripening, and we gleaned some of the leavings. I milked cows into the bowl she held. And I shared with her berries and mushrooms and nuts, which she saw for the first time as they grew and not as they came to table.

It could not last. Her husband had been seeking her through all those months. We had kept ahead of him, travelling in lands whose lords were no friends of his. But in the end, as I knew he would, he and his men caught up with us.

THE LABYRINTH OF THE HEART

"So come saddle me my best black horse,
Come saddle it quite swiftly O,
So I may search for my own wedded wife
Who is gone with the blackguarded gypsies O."

So he rode east and he rode west,
Till he came to yonder boggie-O,
There he spied the pretty young girl
Wi' the gypsies standing around her-O.

They seized me and my brothers. The Earl spoke to his lady: "Come back with me to your proper place. Remember who you are."

And I spoke too. "Yes, my love, you have no choice now but to go back with him. Go to your proper place, and, above all, remember who you are." The Earl thought I had accepted defeat; the fool did not understand me. But I could tell that she knew what I meant — I saw the bubble of merriment on her lips underneath her sadness at what would happen to me, that she could not prevent. The memory of her face as she rode away will stay with me the rest of my few days.

Them seven gypsies all in a row,
They were so brisk and bonnie O,
Tonight they're all condemned to die
For stealing Earl Cassilis' lady O.

They will hang us tonight, my brothers and me. The earl will prosper, all his ventures and lands. The common folk will call him "the Lucky Earl". They will cheer as he and his wife ride out together, calling out "Thanks be to the luck of the Earl." He will nod graciously at this tribute to him, and will never notice her grin as she pretends not to know that she is the Luck of the Earl and it is her who the cheers are truly for.

The earl will never realise that his own poems are deeper than they used to be, that they are no longer rigidly ordered, still less why this is so. He will listen to songs of the minstrels without realising who wrote them, and why they ring with the wild freedom that comes with a gypsy's knowledge of the land.

And he will never know who slips from her bed on May Eve and dances among the corn that the harvest shall be good, nor who leaves her bed at full moon and milks the cows to be sure their milk shall be rich and plentiful.

She will mourn my death. But I die satisfied that she has answered the questions my songs posed her. She has taken my heart, she has joined in the dance, and at last she knows Who she is.

THE DANCER AND THE DANCE

It must have been over fifty years ago that it happened. I was a young man then, and was the best man at a friend's wedding one Midsummer Eve. It was a great party, plenty of food and dancing. Good booze too, but that was the trouble. People were drinking so much that the wine ran out.

As best man, I had to be sure the party didn't fizzle out, so I and another man went down the road to get some more to drink. It wasn't far, just down the road past the green hillock.

We were bringing the drink back, when I heard some music. It seemed to come from the hillock, and sure enough when we got close to it there turned out to be a door open in the hillside, and crowds of people dancing.

I saw at the entrance a young woman with golden hair, which seemed to have a green tinge to it that matched the light green of her dress. She invited me in to join the dance.

Well, you know me. Even now I try to dance when fiddles or flutes are playing fast music. In those days I was a dancing fool and could never resist a dance. One I danced with such fervour that the musicians said that I had danced till they had no energy left for playing.

So I accepted the invitation, and left my companion to carry all the drink himself, though he urged me to remember the party we had come from. I danced with that young woman, both as a couple and in sets. And then I danced with a tall red-haired woman wearing dark green, who seemed to be the centre of the gathering, the ruler of those people, and the heart of the dance.

Suddenly I noticed an old woman sitting by the fire. I could see her fingers and feet tapping to the music, and thought she would have loved to dance if she had been younger. So when the music changed to a very slow tune, I went over and asked her to be my partner. As I had thought, she was a wonderful dancer, moving slowly but performing intricate steps that were almost too much for me to respond to.

Shortly after, the lady of the dance offered me some food. The food and the drink looked wonderful, but I had eaten and drunk so much at my friend's wedding that I refused. She asked me several times, but my stomach could take no more, and I continued to refuse. I thought she looked a little annoyed, perhaps also disappointed, but she finally said, "Well, as you're so sure, I won't offer again tonight."

I continued dancing, first with one then another. My head was in such a whirl that at times I couldn't tell if I was dancing with the young woman, or the old one, or with the great red-haired hostess.

DANIEL COHEN

Suddenly I felt a pull at my sleeve. My companion had taken the drinks to the wedding party and had come back for me. "Come away" he said. "Come away quickly." "What's the hurry" I replied "Another few minutes dancing won't harm me." As he continued to pull me away I wondered why he had stuck his penknife into the door-frame, and why he was looking anxiously at it.

Finally he pulled me out of the dance and through the door, taking his penknife out, and I was angry with him for doing so. "You could have let me dance longer," I said, looking at the hillock in which no door was now visible. "I'd have come back in a short while." "A short while" he said scornfully, "It is a year and a day since you left the wedding, and no-one had any idea how to find you. It's lucky you didn't eat or drink anything. If you had, then you would have had to stay there for ever and I wouldn't have been able to rescue you." But to me it seemed that his action had not been a rescue.

I am glad to have lived my life under the sun and moon, finding love and friendship and also sadness and pain. I would not have wished to have stayed for ever in that twilit world, to lose human contact for ever. And it has often been said to me that the folk of that land live long lives and then just fade into air, that they have no hope of Heaven.

I'm old now, and after many years of living my memory keeps going back to that night when I danced better than I had done ever before or since. My mind sometimes dwells on the young woman who first invited me to dance, at other times on the great stately woman who was ruler of that land, and at yet others on the old woman whose feet knew every dance step there ever was and ever would be. The words of the lady of the dance resonate in my mind. She did not say that she would not offer me food again, but that she "would not offer it again **tonight**." Despite the warnings others have given, you can be sure that I will not refuse when she next offers me food and keeps the promise she made me so long ago.

DANIEL COHEN

THE STORY OF THE STORY (completed)

And so the Story coiled and uncoiled like a great serpent winding around and in between the many worlds. In one coil humans spoke of such fabulous monsters as the unicorn, while in another unicorns thought that human beings were not real but were only fabulous monsters. In one coil those tales (part fantasy, part true) that make up the Matter of France told of the Emperor Charlemagne and his paladins, while in another the Matter of France told of the Emperor Napoleon and his marshals.

After more years than could be counted all the little stories had been told and lived, and the Story was at last complete.

And it murmured happily to itself:
THE END

THE LABYRINTH OF THE HEART

DANIEL COHEN

NOTES ON THE MYTHS

These notes give more information about the background of my stories, and the traditional versions. The booklist suggests several books on the myths.

I often jump about in a collection of stories, rather than reading it from beginning to end. To help others who like to do this, some of the information is repeated when the same characters occur in more than one story.

The Heart of the Labyrinth

The first part **is** how they tell the story.

According to the myth, Ariadne gave Theseus the thread so that he would not get lost in the labyrinth. But the traditional shape of the Cretan labyrinth is not a puzzle maze with dead-ends. It is a single path which twists and turns back on itself in a manner which is confusing but in which one can't get lost.

This pattern is known worldwide. It appears on coins from Crete (approximately a millennium later than the time of the major Cretan culture, though), in India, and is a sacred symbol among the Hopi of North America. More complicated versions appear on the floor of Chartres Cathedral in France. In England, there are several ancient labyrinths cut as brick paths in the turf, the most accessible of which is in Saffron Walden, Essex. In the United States, labyrinths have recently been created on canvas, which can be moved from place to place, the first of which was made for Grace Cathedral, San Francisco.

It is a powerful meditative tool. The twists of its paths can shake up the relationship between the outer world and one's inner self. I have walked, run, danced, and even crawled labyrinths, and always found it a profound experience. Small ones on a page can be followed with the eye or finger.

There is a labyrinth carved on a stone, which may have been a marker on a path for pilgrims, now in the National Museum of Ireland. This story, the first I wrote, developed after meditating on that labyrinth.

The Great Goddess of Crete had 'mistress of the labyrinth' as one of her titles. The name Ariadne means 'utterly pure', which seems to be a name of the Goddess, perhaps in her Moon aspect or even in her Sun aspect — the name may have been used later for priestesses. Janet McCrickard points out in *Eclipse of the Sun* that the solar aspects of the Goddess have been much neglected, as does Shena McGrath in *The Sun Goddess*. The word Minotaur just means 'Bull of Minos'; his name was Asterion, 'starry one'. (Reference: *Dionysus* by Kerenyi).

DANIEL COHEN

Face of Wisdom, Face of Dread

Perseus is usually shown killing Medusa, and being given help by Athene and Hermes. He got information from the Graiae by stealing their single eye and tooth.

One of the names applied to the goddess Athene was 'Gorgon-faced'. This was supposed to be because she carried the head of Medusa on her shield; I suggest a different reason.

The name Medusa means 'ruler', which seems an unlikely name for a monster. If you have seen the Cretan plates and vases decorated with an octopus (still made for tourists, sometimes based on ancient designs) you might feel, as I do, that the octopus and its waving tentacles looks very like a face with waving snake-like hair. Perhaps Medusa was named 'ruler' because she was the Goddess of the Sea in the form of an octopus.

Maiden and Monster

Her name means 'ruler of men'. The story of Perseus, Andromeda, and the monster from the sea later became the story of St. George and the dragon (they even took place in the same town!). This is one of the stories that feminists have had most fun in rewriting; for instance, *Perseus and Andromeda* in Suniti Namjoshi's *Feminist Fables* and a retelling, on a British radio program, by Jenjoy Silverbirch. Also, on a poster for a fund-raising event, and in the *Goddess* issue, which they produced, of *Shrew* magazine, the Matriarchy Study Group, one of the first Goddess groups in Great Britain, showed a "Maiden escaping from Saint George with the aid of a friendly dragon".

In Christian times, the dragon has been seen as a symbol of evil. However, 'dragon' comes from a Greek word meaning 'to see clearly', so perhaps dragons are originally oracular beasts.

Circe's Bard

The story of Odysseus and Circe is much as I have told it. Circe is usually described as an enchantress, who turned Odysseus's men into swine. He himself, arriving later, was protected by the herb moly, which was given to him by Hermes. Odysseus forced Circe to return his men to their normal shape — much to the annoyance of some of them!

I don't have a high opinion of Odysseus; somehow his diplomacy and cleverness remind me of the former US Secretary of State Henry Kissinger. The clever man in *The Biggest Dung-Heap in the World* also reminds me of Odysseus — that's just the kind of way he would think. But others have a kinder feeling towards him.

The bard does not occur in the Greek story. The story I tell of him is based on the Welsh tale of Ceridwen and Taliesin, which can be found in the *Mabinogion*, a collection of Welsh myths. It seemed to fit very well into this setting, partly because Circe was famous for transforming men into animals. The chase with its series of transformations comes from that story. A longer version, with the sexes reversed, is found in the traditional ballad of *The Two Magicians*, also known as *The Coal-Black Smith*, which is number 44 in Francis James Child's great collection *The English and Scottish Popular Ballads* — this ballad has been sung by Martin Carthy, Steeleye Span, and A. L. Lloyd. A similar, but less explicit, theme is found in the folk-song *Hares on the Mountain*.

The meaning of the name Ceridwen is obscure; the best guess seems to be that it means 'holy love'; the ending 'wen' means white. Ceridwen possessed a cauldron in which she brewed the liquor of inspiration. All these matters have become part of my story. The child who was born to Circe is, of course, Homer, who, according to tradition, was blind. There are a series of ancient songs in honour of the Goddesses and Gods that are known as the Homeric Hymns — much of our information about Greek deities comes from these songs.

The Ferryman

The dead are rowed across the river Styx to Hades by the ferryman Charon. The custom of putting coins on a dead person's eyes arises from a need to pay the ferryman's fee. Some living people have crossed, and the ferryman tells us about them.

The passenger is myself — this is a report, to the best of my memory, of what the ferryman said to me.

Other characters in the story (the episodes mentioned come from various myths) are as follows.

The Queen is Persephone, queen of the Underworld. The mention of her attitude to the Big Man means that she also has some aspects of Hera. This fits in with the modern approach, which the Greeks mostly did not follow, of regarding different goddesses as aspects of one. Also "I am all that was, is, and ever will be" is an inscription found in the temple of the Egyptian goddess Neith at Philae.

That the Great Goddess incorporates love, rage, despair and much besides is well expressed by Rosemary Sutcliff, in her historical novel *The Mark of the Horse Lord*, where one character points out that the Great Mother is present both at moments of joy and conception and at moments of destruction and death.

Her universal presence is also stated by Laurell Hamilton in her fantasy novel *A Stroke of Midnight*:

"I did not know that Andais still spoke with you, Goddess."

"I did not stop speaking to my people, they stopped listening to me, and after a time, they could no longer hear my voice. But I never stopped speaking to them. In dreams, or that moment between waking and sleep, there is my voice. In a song, in the touch of another's hand in theirs, I am there. I am Goddess, I am everywhere, and in everything. I cannot leave, nor can you lose me. But you can leave me, and you can turn your back on me."

And Russell Hoban, in his strange and wonderful post-apocalyptic novel *Riddley Walker*, shows an aspect of the Great Goddess when he writes:

"Every thing has a shape and so does the nite only you cant see the shape of nite nor you cant think it. If you put yourself right you can know it. Not with knowing in your head but with the 1st knowing.
...
She has diffrent ways she shows herself. Shes that same 1 shows her moon self or she jus shows her old old nite and no moon. Shes that same 1 every thing and all of us come out of. Shes what she is. Shes a woman when shes Nite and shes a woman when shes Death. The night bearths the day. Every day has the shape of the nite what it come out of. The man as knows that shape can go in to the nite in the nite and the nite in the day time. The woman as knows that shape can be the nite and take the day in her and bearth the new day."

The Warrior is Achilles (the Ten Years' War is, of course, the Trojan War). In the *Odyssey*, when Odysseus calls up his ghost, he gloomily says what I have quoted.

See the notes to *The Singer's Lost Love* to understand why I do not identify the musician with Orpheus.

The Athenian is Theseus. He is recorded as carrying off the Amazon queen Hippolyta, and attempting with a friend, both drunk, to carry off Persephone. In Shakespeare's *A Midsummer Night's Dream*, Bottom the weaver and his friends perform a play for the wedding of Theseus and Hippolyta, and Theseus calls them 'rude mechanicals'.

The Big Man is Heracles; see the notes to *The Biggest Dung-Heap in the World*. He did rescue Theseus and his friend. The ferryman mentions a time when Heracles had almost been tricked. This refers to the occasion when he asked the Titan Atlas, who carried the sky on his shoulders, for assistance. Atlas asked Heracles to take the weight while he gave the help. On his return he intended to leave Heracles carrying the sky, but Heracles tricked him into taking it back.

The dog is the three-headed Cerberus, who guards the gates of Hades.

The Biggest Dung-Heap in the World

As the story is told, the goddess Hera was an enemy of the hero Heracles (who is better known by his Roman name of Hercules) and arranged for him to be set many dangerous tasks. But the name Heracles means 'glory of Hera'. This suggests that in an earlier version of the myth he performed the tasks in her service. The origin of the word 'hero' is unknown, but it does seem possible that it is connected with Hera, and that heroes were originally men dedicated to the service of Hera.

Happy the Land that Needs No Heroes

"Unhappy the land that has no heroes," says a character in Bertolt Brecht's play *Galileo*. "No," replies another. "Unhappy the land that needs heroes."

A very different attitude to heroes from that in most of the stories. This developed from a workshop where we playing with the story of Perseus. It was held at a time when information about tortures in Chile, Argentina and South Africa were in the newspapers. I had been wondering what would have happened if the Graiae had refused to tell Perseus, and I suddenly made the connection. All too often those who torture or commit other crimes in support of a government are regarded as heroes saving society from anarchy.

The First Casualty of War

The myth is much as I have given it. There are many possible ways of answering the question I ask.

Jungians might answer "Agamemnon's [or men's] feminine side." A more political answer, following Riane Eisler, in her book *The Chalice and the Blade* and elsewhere, would be men's participation in a partnership culture. My own preference would be Agamemnon's [or men's] sense of compassion and sense of connectedness with others.

I feel uncomfortable with that Jungian answer, as I don't believe our characteristics fit neatly into feminine and masculine ones. I vividly remember a workshop during which we were asked to identify our strongest masculine and feminine aspects. On that occasion — other occasions might well lead to different answers — my answer was the reverse of what convention would suggest. I was clear that my strongest masculine aspect was that of being nurturing while my strongest feminine aspect was fierceness. I am reminded that the two great heroes of Irish myth, Cuchulain and Finn MacCool, both obtained their training as warriors from women.

I once heard Marina Warner (author of *From the Beast to the Blonde* and other books) remark, in a talk on Circe and transformation, that little girls in ballet classes are encouraged to be butterflies or horses, not tigers. Musing on this and the notion of fierceness as feminine, led me to write the little story below.

THE BALLET CLASS
For Marina Warner, with thanks for her talk about Circe, 27 January 1999

Tillie never liked going to her ballet class.

"I can't understand it," her mother said. "She so enjoys watching ballet on TV. And she's always twirling and dancing around the house."

"Miss Jenkins is so silly, mum," Tillie explained. "She's always trying to get us to dance like a butterfly. I'd rather dance like a Tillie."

So off she went, grumbling as usual.

She cheered up when the class started. Those exercises were hard work but fun. And she enjoyed some of the dancing.

But then the trouble began, as she knew it would. "Let's pretend we are horses," Miss Jenkins exclaimed. "We can gallop away into the distance."

Tillie just stood there, making occasional movements with her feet. "That child has NO imagination," thought Miss Jenkins.

And then it got worse. "Now let's all be tigers."

"Won't" muttered Tillie.

"Come on, Tillie. You can do it. It'll be fun."

"I WON'T," yelled Tillie. "You can't make me."

"Don't be hysterical, child." "Now, tigers everyone. That means YOU, Tillie," Miss Jenkins added brightly.

When the police arrived, the children were still screaming. "I TOLD her" exclaimed Tillie "She wouldn't listen. She MADE me."

The policemen looked down at Miss Jenkins' body, with its head some distance away. "What can have happened," one of them said. "I don't know," said the other, "But it's odd how it reminds me of a mouse after my cat has got it."

The Sleeping Beauty

"There is also a tale for women." There are many traditional tales with a woman or girl as hero. Some of these can be found in James Riordan's *The Woman in the Moon* and Ethel Johnston Phelps's *The Maid of the North*, as well as in more recent collections. One of the first stories I heard as a child, the Scandinavian story *East of the Sun and West of the Moon* is one of these (as is the very similar *The Brown Bull of Norroway*), with the woman going on a quest to find her lover who has been taken from her. I am also very fond of *Kate Crackernuts*, which has been retold by Katherine Briggs. I would love to see a feminist, perhaps a lesbian, retelling of this story, with its very strong relationship between the two Kates and where the princes are only present to provide an excuse for one Kate's adventures.

"The spell ... was cast many years ago by one of your forefathers." In the previous story I ask who was the first casualty of the Trojan war. The quest is to awaken and recover that which has been lost among men for many years, in whatever form each man sees this most clearly.

The specifics of the quest will be different for each man. It can involve explicit political action, therapy, consciousness-raising, and many other forms. I am sure that some men will give up the effort, and that we all will follow false paths from time to time, will have to retrace our steps, and that even if we know what we want to do there are bound to be difficulties, back-trackings, and struggles against oneself.

The transformations when the maiden awakes are based on the traditional story of *The Marriage of Sir Gawain* which I tell next. Women are so often seen by men as beautiful only if they are young. Here the final transformation is to the full beauty and power of a 'woman of your own age'. This, depending on the individual man, may of course be a young woman, an old one, or a woman who is mature and not young or old. The three aspects of Sleeping Beauty correspond to the three faces of the Goddess, most often referred to as Maiden, Mother, and Crone, but sometimes described as Maiden, Queen, and Crone. I prefer the second naming, as it places less emphasis on fertility. It is also important not to regard youth as an essential feature of beauty, as is so often done by men and even by women. Equally, an old person (man or woman) may think of themselves as 'young inside'. This can be very rewarding, giving people the opportunity to do things they might otherwise think unsuitable, but still places the priority on youth.

"For what she demands of you is nothing less than strength, majesty and love to equal her own." This is a great and frightening demand. Most feminists, when they criticise men, hold that men can change their behaviour and must do so for a just society to be created. There are some feminists, but very few, who take the view that men are essentially no good. To me, this seems to let men off lightly. If we men are essentially no good, then we can never change our nature, so why bother to try. The challenge is to respond to the cry that men are not as good as we can be, and the call to be the best we are capable of. This is expressed by Asphodel Long at the end of her essay on *Politics of Sexuality* (first published in *Politics of Matriarchy* (Matriarchy Study Group 1979), now available on her Web site at www.asphodel-long.com).

I think this story could be used for guided meditations. I have much experience of taking part in such meditations, but I have not led any. So I leave the details of how this can be done to readers who have led meditations. I would be glad to hear from anyone who does use the story in that way.

What Women Most Desire

There are many versions of this tale, the best known of which is the one Chaucer told in *The Canterbury Tales* as the *Wife of Bath's Tale*. The different versions of the story give related, but significantly different, versions of the answer to the question "What do women most desire?" Some versions are very anti-women, with an answer such as "Power over men". The answer I give is very like the one in the ballad version of *The Marriage of Sir Gawain* (number 31 in *The English and Scottish Popular Ballads*). The death of Gawain's wife is found in several versions. The suggestion that this was in childbirth, and Gawain's response to this, is my own. I was influenced by Starhawk, who pointed out in *The Spiral Dance* (p.46) that pregnancy and birth has always carried with it the risk of death.

The Singer's Lost Love

This is based on the story of Orpheus and Eurydice. Eurydice is usually shown as dying from a snakebite. Orpheus reclaims her as in my story. He is warned not to look at her until they are back in the open air. He loses her because he looks when he is out, but she, being a few paces behind him, is not.

Orpheus absolutely refused to lend his name to the story. He told me that he had learned more understanding than the singer I wrote of. In the story as it is usually told Eurydice is a nymph. But her name means 'wide justice' or 'wide custom' (the suggestion by Rushdie of 'wide ruler' is based on a secondary meaning of the Greek word *dike*), a name which is most fitted to the Queen of the Underworld. My suggestion as to what happens when he looks back seems natural once this identification is made. My story was written before Salman Rushdie's modern-day version of the story of Orpheus and Eurydice, *The Ground Beneath her Feet*. In Chapter 16 of that book, Rushdie reaches very similar conclusions.

The unity of dark and light and the need for sorrow as well as joy are themes in several of my stories. I have taken to heart William Blake's remarks in his poem *Auguries of Innocence*:

> Man was made for Joy and Woe;
> And when this we rightly know
> Thro' the World we safely go.
> Joy & Woe are woven fine,
> A Clothing for the Soul divine;
> Under every grief & pine
> Runs a joy with silken twine.

Of Power, Good Counsel, and Wisdom

This is a version of the birth of Athene. When Metis (the name can reasonably be translated as 'Good Counsel') was pregnant by Zeus ('Power' in my story) it was prophesied that if she had a son he would supersede Zeus. In fear of this he swallowed her. In due course Athene (goddess of Wisdom) was born, and emerged through Zeus's head. In the play *The Furies* by Aeschylus (the third part of the *Oresteia* — the play is also called *The Eumenides*, a Greek word that means "Kindly Ones"), she has a speech claiming that a child is related only to its father, not its mother, giving as a justification her own birth from a father alone.

In the Jewish and Christian traditions, Wisdom (Hochma in Hebrew, Sophia in Greek) is a female figure who is an aspect of deity. This has been forgotten for many years, but people are beginning to re-discover Her. This discovery in the outside world, and the implications that people are beginning to find in this, gives me hope that She will return to govern the world as in my story. Scriptural and modern accounts of Her may be found in *In a Chariot Drawn by Lions* by Asphodel Long and *The Wisdom of Fools* by Mary Grey, among others.

In the biblical book of Proverbs, it is said (Chapters 8 and 3):

The Lord created me at the beginning of his work, The first of his acts of old…

When he established the heavens I was there…

When he assigned to the sea its limits, when he marked out the foundations of the earth,

Then I was beside him …

Her ways are pleasant ways, and her paths all lead to prosperity.

She is a tree of life to those who grasp her, and those who hold fast to her are safe.

And in the biblical Book of Wisdom of Solomon (which is in the Catholic bible, but in Protestant bibles occurs in the texts known as the Apocrypha which are often omitted), we are told:

She is so pure she pervades and permeates all things…
She is but one, yet can do all things; herself unchanging, she makes all things new…
She spans the world in power from end to end, and gently orders all things.
In kinship with Wisdom is immortality, and in friendship with her pure delight.

Esmeralda's Quest

This piece, about the power of stories, begins a change of direction, as many of the later stories depend less directly than the earlier ones on traditional myths and folktales. The main themes remain present, however.

Like so many of my stories, this had its origin in a workshop led by Hugh Lupton and Eric Maddern. In it, we had to create a personal myth out of aspects of our lives. Esmeralda had attended the workshop and insisted that she needed her own myth told, so here it is.

The stories that she heard and learnt can be found in many books of folktales, for adults and children. Thomas the Rhymer's story can be heard as a ballad, or read in a novel by Ellen Kushner. Sir Gawain's marriage is an earlier story in this book (*What Women Most Desire*), while his playing of the beheading game is the heart of the poem of *Gawain and the Green Knight*. *Beowulf* is a famous Anglo-Saxon poem, perhaps best known in the version by Seamus Heaney, though there is also an excellent version by Kevin Crossley-Holland. The story of the castle *East of the Sun and West of the Moon* comes from Scandinavia (and is one of the descendants of the tale of Cupid and Psyche). Baba Yaga appears in many Russian tales; I was thinking particularly of the story of *Vasilissa the Fair*. My father told me the story of the king of the cats when I was very young; different versions name him differently, but I was told that his name was Milman.

Finally, I will add another story coming from a different workshop, on writing and traditional tales led by Kevin Crossley-Holland and Malachy Doyle. It is a twist on a Mongolian tale of a man who chose to seek Death, and the reward he got, and was also sparked by a remark that adverbs kill stories.

ONE WHO MET DEATH, A STORY

The stories were dying. No-one was telling them any more. True, people were writing them in books and other people were reading them. But that is a poor thing compared to the energy a story gets when it dances from speaker to listener and back again.

The writers would have been horrified if they had learnt what many of them were doing. They thought they were bringing stories they loved to a wider audience. Indeed they were doing this, and it was necessary and valuable, but it was little more than sustaining invalids rather than restoring them to health. And too many of them were killing the stories, stabbing them with sharp adverbs or crushing them with heavy adverbs.

One story decided not to wait until death came to it, but to make its own path to the land of the dead. It travelled to the heart of cities, to the depths of the country, to ships on the wild and stormy seas, seeking out those who told it. Carefully, cautiously, unnoticeably (in better words, avoiding the damaging adverbs, exercising great care and caution to avoid being noticed), it withdrew itself from them.

At last only one man knew the story, and he was old and near to death.

The story stayed with the man as he lay dying, accompanying him on his final journey.

"How are you here?" asked Death, "It is not your time."

"It may not be the time you chose for meeting me" replied the story, "but it is the time I chose for meeting you."

"Nevertheless, it is not your time, and you must return. But for your bravery, I will give you a gift."

The story looked at many gifts. It could return with the gift of laughter, to make all who heard it fill with merriment. It could return with the gift of tears, to make all who heard it weep for the sadness of the world. The gift of sleep, the gift of calm, and many others it looked at.

At last it decided. "Let me return with a storyteller. He can decide whether laughter, tears, or sleep are called for."

Death put his hand on the man with whom the story had travelled.

"But he is too old" objected the story.

"Oh, he won't be back in the form in which he came here. And you will have to wait for your storyteller."

On its return, the story found itself in the mind of a baby who had no words. Then in the mind of a child, who did not have enough words to tell the story. Then in the mind of a boy, who knew the words of the story but did not understand it.

As it waited, it realised that other stories were joining it, some that Death had sent back, others who had come of their own accord.

As the boy became a young man, he started telling stories, at first just to family and friends, then to larger audiences. Mostly, the listeners simply enjoyed themselves and said afterwards that it had been a good entertainment. But from time to time someone listening to a story would spark with recognition and say "I want that story." As more and more people claimed stories, so the stories became stronger.

And as people began telling stories again, the stories were alive and healthy once more.

The Interpreter

The Greek god Hermes, trickster and lord of language, likes puns. This story had its origin in the pun in the last line and the subtitle. Hermes is also the god of thieves, merchants, and diplomacy, and wears winged sandals and carries a staff with snakes. The story includes all these aspects.

The word 'hermeneutics' is from a Greek word meaning 'interpreter', which in turn is derived from the role of Hermes as deity of speech, writing, and trade. It is the art of interpretation, especially of the scriptures. The account given in the story does cover some basic hermeneutical techniques. Some of the ideas in the story were suggested by two of Elizabeth Schussler Fiorenza's academic books on feminist hermeneutics, *But SHE Said* and *Bread, not Stone*.

Rabbi Malka Drucker (in the July 1st, 2003, issue of the online magazine *Awakened Woman*) expresses the idea that every text contains two messages by saying: "An ancient Jewish commentary describes sacred text as "black fire written upon white fire." Black tells one story, white another. We can only read the first story, but one day we will know both narratives, and on that day, when we have the whole story, we'll know how to live in peace." She suggests that the white fire, the part that has been neglected, is "the other story, the "white fire" that reveals the divine through women's lives as creators and nurturers of life."

I discovered two relevant quotations after I had begun the story, which I feel was a gift from Hermes. The sentences "But then I read ...to be received" are by Lynn Gottlieb (*The Secret Jew* in *On Being A Jewish Feminist*), while the passage about landfolk is a paraphrase of a passage in A.S. Byatt's *Angels and Insects* (at the end of Chapter V of *The Conjugal Angel*). Byatt is the "wise woman" the interpreter refers to.

Rimble, the Trickster god who is the central character of Zohra Greenhalgh's fantasy novel, *Contrarywise*, asked me to be sure to mention his favourite notion, that of an 'Improoovement'. I wanted to pay homage to this other trickster god by using this word rather than just referring to an 'improvement'.

In Arthur Conan Doyle's *The Memoirs of Sherlock Holmes*, in the case of *Silver Blaze*, we find the following remarks.

"[I draw your attention to] the curious incident of the dog in the night-time."

"The dog did nothing in the night-time."

"That was the curious incident," remarked Sherlock Holmes.

Though this occurred far distant in time and place from the city of our story, it is very like the interpreter's insistence that we pay attention to what is omitted from a text as well as to what is included.

The controversy over sailors and their role in the temple was suggested by the controversy in the Church of England over ordination of women.

Do you think the story is too male-dominated, with its mention of farmers, merchants, and sailors? If so, use some hermeneutical analysis. The only character whose gender is mentioned is the interpreter himself.

New Shoes for New Weather

This arose from a story-telling workshop on the theme of shoes. We were given fabric, beads, paper, paint, and other materials with which we made a pair of shoes, and many of us created winged sandals. I felt the presence of Hermes, who wears winged sandals for speed, and is lord of language, in the workshop, and this story is my acknowledgement of his presence.

He is also lord of trade and of thievery, and a guide to the land of the dead. All these attributes have their place in the story. The phone company that gave cheap rates was called 'Mercury' — Mercury is the Roman god corresponding to the Greek Hermes. Even the mention of someone who would "thunder at him with all his might" is an acknowledgement by Hermes of the ruler of the Greek gods, Zeus, known as the Thunderer.

The title comes from a song written by Nancy Nicholson. It can be found on the record *I Heard a Woman Singing* by Frankie Armstrong, a great singer of the British folk revival, equally at home in traditional ballads, humorous songs, and political songs.

A Successful Experiment?

Up to the point where Loki gives a reason for refusing to weep, this follows the myth. Most versions say that the mistletoe was overlooked because it was so small and weak, which does not feel a good enough reason. I have known from my childhood the suggestion that the mistletoe was not included because it could not be classified one way or the other. Boundaries and thresholds have traditionally always been places of magic and power.

Loki's rude remarks to the gods, and his praise of Sif, fit with what we know of him. There is a whole poem of such remarks, translated, in the books *The Elder Edda* and *Norse Poems*, by W. H. Auden under the title *Loki's Flyting*.

"Oh the cleverness of me," is a typical Loki remark, but it was actually said by Peter Pan in J. M. Barrie's play of that name.

His claim to have created the universe may just have been to confuse the other gods, a typical Loki trick. There's no evidence of his claim in the myths. But trickster gods in other cultures have also been creators. I heard from Dovie Thomason, a Lakota/Kiowa storyteller, a traditional saying regarding the trickster Coyote, that "We are all Coyote's children."

For another positive approach to Loki, see the children's book *The Eight Days of Luke* by Diana Wynne Jones.

Taste and See

The first quote and the title are taken, with permission, from the song *Taste and See* on Betsy Rose's cassette of songs, *In My Two Hands*, based on the teachings of Thich Nhat Hanh and Creation Spirituality. Psalms 34:8 says 'Taste and see that the Lord is good.'

The second quote is an eighteenth century version of a remark by the twelfth century theologian and bishop Peter Lombard.

A discussion of the ancient and modern uses of midrash can be found in an article by David Stern in *The Jewish Study Bible*.

We are told (Genesis, chapter 2, verse 20) that Adam named the animals. Someone must have named the plants, but no details are given, so my story suggests that Eve named them.

Genesis does not say what fruit the Tree of Knowledge produced. It is commonly regarded as being an apple, but this may simply be because the Latin word for apple is *malus* and that for evil is *malum*. Some rabbinical writings suggest that the fruit was a fig.

Readers may wonder why there is no serpent in my telling. One reason is that I am telling the story from Adam's viewpoint, and he does not know of the serpent until very late on. Another reason is that the serpent's role and motivations are so important that they could take over any story. But the primary reason is that the serpent chose not to be present.

Some of the details that readers may find surprising in my version can be found in rabbinic or theological commentaries on the story. Those interested in these details can find references in the original publication of this story in *Patriarchs, Prophets and Other Villains*.

A version of the story of Adam and Eve that particularly appeals to me as a storyteller has been told by Jean Houston. In my words to her version, it runs as follows:

God looked down at the Garden of Eden, and sighed deeply. His best friend, known to us as Satan, asked what was the matter.

"I can't understand it," said God. "I've told them and told them not to eat of that tree, and what happens."

"What does happen?"

"Nothing, that's the problem."

"Let me see what I can do," replied Satan. And he went off to the Garden in the form of a serpent, with the results that we all know.

God was happy. "**Now** the story can begin."

The Man who did not Like Spiders

The information on spiders comes from various sources, both scientific and mythological (W.S. Bristowe. *The World of Spiders*. I first heard of Dr. Thomas Muffet from *The Oxford Dictionary of Nursery Rhymes* — the nursery rhyme of *Little Miss Muffet* is supposed to be based on his daughter.

I learnt from Bristowe's book that there are over 35000 kinds of spiders, whose sizes range from one-twentyfifth of an inch to over ten inches.

Insects have six legs and some can fly. Arachnids, which, in addition to spiders, include scorpions and mites, have eight legs and cannot fly, and it is not surprising that the spiders object to the confusion. Many of us make this mistake, but Dr. Muffet should have known better than to have included them in a book whose title referred to insects.

Many Native American peoples have stories about Spider Woman or Grandmother Spider. The story of how Spider brought fire is Cherokee, while the other two I mentioned are Hopi.

This story, surprisingly, developed from an exercise on wounding and healing at a workshop on the Grail. During that exercise I saw myself stung by a spider and placed in a cocoon.

I have always liked spiders.

The Mathematician who had Little Wisdom.

I was by profession a mathematician. This story was written when I was at a conference in Edinburgh. What happened to the hero of the story is in part an account of a genuine mathematical result that came from my own research. I would have liked to give a more detailed explanation of the result as part of the story, but it would have required so much information that the story itself would have been swamped.

At that conference I presented the mathematical result, together with its technical details, the form of this story rather than as an academic paper. This bringing together of my interest in mathematics and stories felt the climax of my mathematical career, and a good beginning to my retirement.

The Salmon of Wisdom comes from Celtic myth, but the general plot line comes from a well-known folk-tale sometimes called *The Fisherman and his Wife* or *The Flounder*.

In the question period after I had given the talk, I told the traditional tale of Finn MacCool and the Salmon of Wisdom, which I include here.

The druid Finnegas was sitting by the river Shannon, fishing for the Salmon of Wisdom, as he had often done. But he had seen that it was the day the Salmon would be caught, and that when one named Finn ate it he would gain wisdom.

At last he caught it and lovingly prepared a fire on which to bake it. He called for his student, who was known as Deimne, to look after the cooking for him. The young man was happy to do so.

He placed it on a dish to serve it to Finnegas. But then he noticed that there was a blister on its skin, which spoiled its appearance, and he decided to press it down with his thumb. The salmon was still very hot, and he burnt his thumb and put it in his mouth to cool the pain. Instantly he became aware of the movement of fish in the water, of birds in the air, of animals on land, and he knew what they were saying to each other.

When Finnegas tasted the salmon he knew that wisdom was no longer in its flesh. His student told him what had happened. "Is your name truly Deimne?" asked Finnegas.

"No, I am Finn, the son of Cumhail."

"Then the prophecy was for you, not me."

From that day, Finn the son of Cumhail, also known as Finn MacCool, put his thumb in his mouth and chewed on it whenever he had need of knowledge. And he became renowned for his wisdom as well as his bravery.

And, to this day, one sign that that a person is descended from Finn MacCool is that they will put their thumb in their mouth and chew on it whenever they are thinking hard.

Later in the conference, one of my colleagues gave a talk, and was asked a difficult question afterwards. He thought for a while, put his thumb in his mouth and chewed on it, and finally answered. Instead of the usual applause, there was much laughter from the audience. For his name was Jim McCool.

The Ballad of Jack Green

Jack Green in my poem is suggested by Jack-in-the-Green or Green Man, a traditional figure associated with spring. The interpretation of him as the spirit of vegetation and new growth may be ancient, but cannot be reliably traced back further than the nineteenth century. He is discussed in *Green Man* by William Anderson, *The Green Man* by Kathleen Basford, and *Jack-in-the-Green* by Roy Judge. There are many May Day customs and festivals in England, among them the Sweeps Festival in Rochester, Kent, where a Jack-in-the-Green appears, and the Green Man festival in Hastings, Kent — both of these were started in the 1980s as revivals of earlier festivals.

A parallel figure is the spirit of the harvest, who appears in the traditional song *John Barleycorn*, a version of which is given below.

> There were three men come out of the west
> Their fortunes for to try
> And they have made a solemn vow
> John Barleycorn must die
>
> They plowed him in three furrows deep
> Laid clods all on his head
> And they have made a solemn oath
> John Barleycorn was dead
>
> Well then there came a shower of rain
> Which from the clouds did fall
> John Barleycorn sprang up again
> And so amazed them all
>
> Well then came men with great sharp scythes
> To cut him off at the knee
> They bashed his head against a stone
> And they used him barbarously
>
> Well then came men with great long flails
> To cut him skin from bone
> The miller has used him worse than that
> He ground him between two stones
>
> They wheeled him here, they wheeled him there
> Wheeled him into the barn

And they have used him worse than that
They bunged him in a vat

They worked their will upon John Barleycorn
But he lives to tell the tale
We pour him into an old brown jug
And we call him home-brewed ale

The song about Jack-in-the-Green which follows has all the appearance of being traditional, but it was actually written by Martin Graebe in 1972.

Now Winter is over I'm happy to say
And we're all met again in our ribbons so gay
And we're all met again, to rejoice in the spring
And to go about dancing with Jack in the Green
Jack in the Green, Jack in the Green
And we'll all dance each springtime with Jack in the Green

Now Jack in the Green is a very strange man
Though he dies every Autumn he's born every spring
And each year on his birthday, we will dance through the street
And in return Jacky will ripen the wheat
Jack in the Green, Jack in the Green
And we'll all dance each springtime with Jack in the Green

Now all you young maidens I'd have you beware
Of touching young Jack for there's strange powers there
For if you but touch him there is many will tell
Like the wheat in our fields so your belly will swell
Jack in the Green, Jack in the Green
And we'll all dance each springtime with Jack in the Green

With his mantle he'll cover the trees that are bare
Our gardens he'll trim with his jacket so fair
But our fields he will sow with the hair of his head
And the grain it will ripen till old Jack is dead
Jack in the Green, Jack in the Green
And we'll all dance each springtime with Jack in the Green

Now the sun is half up and it signals the hour
That the children arrive with their garlands of flowers
So now let the music and the dancing begin
And touch the good heart of young Jack in the Green
Jack in the Green, Jack in the Green
And we'll all dance each springtime with Jack in the Green

THE LABYRINTH OF THE HEART

Three Worlds, Two Queens, One Prince

Based on the First Branch of the collection of Welsh tales known as the *Mabinogion*. My version follows the story accurately. The speaker is not in the original — but he wanted to tell me what happened. This was created at a storytelling retreat on the *Mabinogion*, run by Hugh Lupton and Eric Maddern.

The Seer in the Hawthorn Tree

This had two origins. One was a mask-making workshop run by my friend Jan Henning, where the mask I made was "man emerging from hawthorn tree". The call to Nimue was written at one of Hugh Lupton and Eric Maddern's storytelling retreats, where we had to create an invocation to a deity from Welsh or Irish tradition.

In the Arthurian stories, Nimue is said to have learned magic from Merlin and then to have imprisoned him. The nature of the prison varies between different stories, sometimes a rock or cave, sometimes a hawthorn tree.

Pity the Poor Emigrant

The first and last verses comprise the poem *Down by the Salley Gardens* by W. B. Yeats. The second and third verses are traditional, the second being best known as sung by Steeleye Span, and the title was suggested by the title of a song by Bob Dylan. This story came from a storytelling retreat, run by Hugh Lupton and Eric Maddern, whose theme was trees. Cards with images of trees were laid out face-down on a table, and we each picked one. The card I was drawn to turned out to be the willow. I didn't like any of the traditional tales about willows, so I created this one, based on poems and songs of lost love.

We worked on an obscure Welsh poem, the *Cad Goddeu* or *Battle of the Trees*. This is translated in *The White Goddess* by Robert Graves. Robin Williamson tells this story in his performances and also in a book which has appeared under two titles, *The Craneskin Bag* and *The Wise and Foolish Tongue*. In this poem the enchanter Gwydion raises up trees to fight for him. We are told that in this battle "The willow was late to the fray." In the workshop we each had to write a poem in the character of our tree, and my poem below explains why the willow was late.

> I hear the call to battle — I shall resist.
> For I have known of battles, I have known of grief.
> Young men conscripted, dragged from their lovers' arms,
> Women mourning through the years of leaf-fall.

I hear the call to battle — let it pass harmlessly through my branches.
Let young men and maidens lick honey from each other's fingers.
Let them like silver trout swim in the gliding stream.
No more shall salt tears water my roots.
No more shall joy destroyed die hanging on my branches.
I hear the call to battle — not willingly do I answer.

Johnny Faa's Indictment

There are many versions of the ballad which is the source of this story, with titles such as *The Gypsy Laddie, Seven Gypsies, The Wraggle-Taggle Gypsies-O, Black Jack Davy*. This is number 200 in Child's *The English and Scottish Popular Ballads*; information about the origin of the story, in particular the name Johnny Faa, can be found there. The verses quoted come from several versions. The first verse is from the singing of Jeannie Robertson, the second and third are from a version in Child, the fourth and seventh from the singing of Jean Redpath, and the fifth, sixth and eighth from the singing of A. L. Lloyd.

According to the singer and storyteller Sheila Stewart, herself of traveller origin, the travelling people of Scotland (often derogatively called tinkers) are of very different background from the gypsies. She says that there were never any gypsies in Scotland, and that Johnnie Faa was a traveller.

The Dancer and the Dance

This is based on a traditional story, told in the 'Fairylore' workshop at an Annual Meeting of the Society for Storytelling. There are many tales of those who were abducted to the Otherworld or chose to go there, and it can be a less pleasant and more dangerous place than I showed it. The best-known are the two ballads of *Thomas the Rhymer* and *Tam Lin*. Good fantasy novels based on these themes are *Thomas the Rhymer* by Ellen Kushner and *Fire and Hemlock* by Diana Wynne Jones. Nancy Springer beautifully describes that world as the land of "Fair Peril" in a fantasy novel of that name (about a storyteller!) and Terry Pratchett's *Lords and Ladies* is an essential warning to those who can only see the glamour of the Folk. A brilliant children's book on the theme of abduction to the Otherworld is *Catkin* by Antonia Barber, illustrated by P. J. Lynch, who I feel sure has seen the Folk.

As I said in the Introduction (following some thoughts of Neil Gaiman and others) it is that world that gives meaning to the everyday world. It is a second home for all storytellers, and many of us have a devotion to the Queen of Elfland (as she is often named).

I avoid the five-letter word beginning with 'f' to describe the beings of that land, as they don't like it. Many people call them "The Good Neighbours", "The Gentry", or by the Irish name of Sidhe or the Welsh name of "Tylwyth Teg" ("People of Peace"). I'm even more cautious, and usually just say "Them" or "Those Folk".

It is said of them (as quoted in *An Encyclopedia of Fairies* by Katherine Briggs):

> Gin ye ca' me imp or elf
> I rede ye look weel to yourself;
> Gin ye ca' me fairy
> I'll work ye muckle tarrie;
> Gin guid neibour ye ca' me
> Then guid neibour I will be;
> But gin ye ca' me seelie wicht
> I'll be your freend both day and nicht.

The Story of the Story

A very short piece called *Imagine* by the fantasy writer Fredric Brown has stuck in my mind for over fifty years, and I think has influenced this story. Lewis Carroll's *Through the Looking Glass* presents a unicorn who thought humans were fabulous monsters until he met Alice. In our world the Matter of France is the name given to the legends about Charlemagne and his paladins (while the Matter of Britain is the name given to the Arthurian stories), but the world of Poul Anderson's fantasy novel *Three Heart and Three Lions* is one in which the Matter of France refers to a legendary Napoleon.

BOOKLIST

Because there are several editions of many of the books I mention, and the UK and US publishers may be different, I give the author and title only, but not the publisher or publication date.

Mythology

Graves, Robert. *The Greek Myths*. The best general reference for the details of the myths. He gives the sources for the stories, and has lengthy notes giving his interpretations for them. His book is a reference book, though, and his interpretations are not generally accepted. For versions of the myths, which are pleasant to read it may be best to look at the retellings intended for children.

Spivey, Nigel. *Songs on Bronze*. An excellent modern retelling of many of the Greek myths.

Warner, Rex. *Men and Gods*. This older book has been recently republished, but his other books on Greek mythology, *Greeks and Trojans* and *The Vengeance of the Gods* (and the omnibus edition, *The Stories of the Greeks*) are still out of print. They are not too difficult to find, and are well-written and intended for adults.

Deary, Terry. *Top Ten Greek Legends*. Intended for children, it is great fun and also accurate; Theseus as reported by the "Sun" tabloid newspaper, the teenage Perseus' diary, how Heracles performs on his Twelve Heroic Aptitude Tests, and others.

Room, Adrian. *Room's Classical Dictionary*. This was my reference for the meanings of various names.

Auden, W. H. and Taylor, Paul. *The Elder Edda*. An accurate poetic translation of one of the main sources for Norse mythology.

Jones, Gwyn and Jones, Thomas. *The Mabinogion*.

Ford, Patrick K. *The Mabinogi, and other medieval Welsh Tales*. The Mabinogion is the main collection of Welsh myths, first translated into English by Lady Charlotte Guest in the mid-nineteenth century. I find the version by Jones and Jones one of the best of many translations.

Walton, Evangeline. *Prince of Annwn*.

Walton, Evangeline. *The Mabinogion Tetralogy*. Walton has written four novels based on the Mabinogion, which are collected in the recent Overlook Press edition. I make specific mention of *Prince of Annwn* because this is based on the myth that I used in *Three Worlds, Two Queens, One Prince*.

Doniger, Wendy. *The Implied Spider*. A dense and difficult book by an academic. But full of elegant writing and profound thinking. A useful counterbalance to the universalist approach to myth of Jung and Campbell. By far the best analysis of myth and its functions that I have come across.

Goddesses

Gadon, Elinor. *The Once and Future Goddess*. There are many books on the ancient goddesses and the cultures that worshipped them, and on spirituality from a feminist standpoint. This book is one of the few I feel able to recommend for someone who is just beginning to become interested in these matters.

Sjoo, Monica and Mor, Barbara. *The Great Cosmic Mother: rediscovering the religion of the earth*. A classic account of goddesses and goddess religion jointly written by an artist who was one of the founders of the Goddess movement in Great Britain and an American poet.

Baring, Anne and Cashford, Jules. *The Myth of the Goddess*. Another good encyclopedic text from a Jungian perspective.

Walker, Barbara. *Women's Encyclopaedia of Myths and Secrets*. This book has a mass of fascinating information, though she does not always make clear when she is making an interpretation of a story or some information and when she is telling the conventional version. It is an ideal book to dip into, and for detailed and reliable accounts one can look at her sources (which are carefully referenced) and even the sources of her sources.

Gimbutas, Marija. *The Goddesses and Gods of Old Europe* (originally published in 1974 under the title *The Gods and Goddesses of Old Europe*).

Gimbutas, Marija. *The Language of the Goddess*.

Gimbutas, Marija. *The Civilization of the Goddess*. These are the three major books on goddesses in prehistory, full of marvellous images as well as much information. Gimbutas was a distinguished archaeologist, but her views on ancient goddesses are rejected by most of her colleagues.

Billington, Sandra and Green, Miranda (eds.). *The Concept of the Goddess*.

Goodison, Lucy and Morris, Christine (eds.). *Ancient Goddesses*. These two books contain essays by archaeologists, anthropologists and other scholars contain much valuable information about goddesses. Their criticisms of Gimbutas need to be read by anyone interested in her work — I think it likely that in the long run much of her later work will be as well-accepted as her earlier work, but this can only happen if her supporters and followers respond to the criticisms. Unfortunately, both books significantly misunderstand the modern Goddess movement — in particular they do not see the dance that moves from "goddesses" to "Goddess" and back again, and from scholarship to imagination and intuition and back, often within one person in the course of a few minutes.

Dexter, Miriam Robbins. *Whence the Goddesses*. A valuable sourcebook, with information about many goddesses (primarily those from ancient Europe, India and Iran), their powers and functions, with extracts from the texts about them.

Christ, Carol. *The Laughter of Aphrodite*. A collection of essays on Goddess theology, including *Reclaiming Goddess History* and the classic *Why Women Need the Goddess*.

Christ, Carol. *The Rebirth of the Goddess*. An attempt at a systematic thealogy of the Goddess. Christian theologians have had two thousand years to develop their ideas, while this is the first book on Goddess thealogy.

Tim Ward. *Savage Breast*. Combines historical and archaeological information about various goddesses with the author's travels to places associated with them. His personal experiences of aspects of the goddess and his relationships with his partner form the heart of a book that is valuable on many levels.

McLean, Malcolm. *Devoted to the Goddess*. A scholarly account of the life and works of Ramprasad, the 18th century Bengali poet and devotee of the goddess Kali. It includes translations of some of the poems.

McDermott, Rachel Fell. *Singing to the Goddess*. A collection of devotional poems from Bengal to the goddesses Kali and Uma. Contains many of Ramprasad's poems.

Hixon, Lex. *Mother of the Universe*. A more popular translation of Ramprasad's poems. This version is particularly readable but probably not as accurate as the previous two books. I much prefer Ramprasad to Rumi or Kabir, who are better known, perhaps because he writes of the divine as a goddess rather than a god. While I admire Rumi, and his writings speak to my mind, Ramprasad speaks to my heart.

Seely, Clinton (translator). *Grace and Mercy in her Wild Hair*. Another very readable translation of Ramprasad.

There are many booklists and resources on the Web, best found by using a search engine and looking for "goddess bibliography" or "goddess mythology".

The Mythopoetic and the Pro-Feminist Men's Movements

Bly, Robert. *Iron John*.

Moore, Robert and Gillette, Douglas. *King, Warrior, Magician, Lover*. These are two classics of the mythopoetic men's movement. Whether one likes them or not, they are necessary reading for anyone wanting to understand that movement.

Meade, Michael. *Men and the Water of Life*. I prefer this to the previous two. Meade spends less time on theory and more on experience, both of the workshops he runs and of his own life. And, unlike Bly, he uses a number of different stories. But there is still little of society in the book, and less about men's relationships with women than I would wish. My main issue with all these books is that they take conventional forms of the stories as definitive, and do not question their choice of stories. The result is that they reinforce conventional views of masculinity and femininity rather than analysing or challenging them.

Doty, William. *Myths of Masculinity*. Not as easy to read as the previous three books, since it is intended as much for gender studies courses as for men's groups. But it tells various myths and analyses their contemporary relevance from a standpoint I am in sympathy with.

Stoltenberg, John. *The End of Manhood*. Stoltenberg argues that "manhood" is an illusion, and that "selfhood" is what men should be seeking. His analysis is acute, and he is aware of social issues. His book is an important corrective to the first three books mentioned, but in the end I feel he has missed something. Perhaps he is still caught in the idea that we are minds who own bodies (so that our form, gender and sexuality are of little relevance to our being), while I feel this dualism is both a cause and a symptom of the patriarchal society we live in.

Chinen, Allan. *Beyond the Hero*. This one tells stories relevant to men who are in midlife, or younger but "caught in the middle", and discusses the stories, mainly from a psychological viewpoint. He holds that the hero is part of a patriarchal tradition, and has to be set aside in maturity. Surprisingly (and refreshingly), the figure he sees as relevant is the trickster.

Mazis, Glen A. *The Trickster, Magician & Grieving Man*. This book combines a social understanding with a mythopoetic one. I would have liked to have written this book.

Rowan, John. *The Horned God*. Rowan is one of the very few people who have worked on each of the social, psychological, and spiritual levels. He sees the need for men to act on all these levels, and his book is a great help for those who want to do so.

Hagan, Kay L. (ed.). *Women Respond to the Men's Movement*. A collection of articles of different women's views of the men's movements, mythopoetic, activist, and others. I responded positively to many of the critiques, but not all. Other men will probably have different likes and dislikes from me, but these views from the outside of the movement need to be taken account of.

Kimmel, Michael. *The Politics of Manhood.* Pro-feminist men respond to the mythopoetic men's movement. Valuable criticism, but the authors do not understand that a mythological approach can be valuable if it is combined with a social and political analysis.

Roscoe, Will. *Queer Spirit: a gay men's myth book.* An interesting collection of myths that are or can be interpreted as being about gay male relationships. What I found most interesting was his general discussion, looking at the effect of mythical connections between similar people, and seeing a reflection in another person, whereas many myths of heterosexuals emphasise difference and complementarity.

Bly, Robert, Hillman, James and Meade, Michael (eds.). *The Rag and Bone Shop of the Heart.* This is a collection of poems which the editors and others have spoken at various men's workshops. It's a marvellous collection for anyone who likes poetry. This book will introduce people to the wonderful mystical poems of Rumi and Kabir, but it does not include my favourite mystical poet, Ramprasad.

Books referred to in the notes (in their order of mention)

McCrickard, Janet. *Eclipse of the Sun.*
McGrath, Shena. *The Sun Goddess.*
Kerenyi, Karl. *Dionysus.*
Namjoshi, Suniti. *Feminist Fables.*
Sutcliff, Rosemary. *The Mark of the Horse Lord.*
Hoban, Russell. *Riddley Walker.*
Hamilton, Laurell. *A Stroke of Midnight.*
Eisler, Riane. *The Chalice and the Blade.*
Riordan, James. *The Woman in the Moon.*
Phelps, Ethel Johnston. *The Maid of the North.*
Briggs, Katherine. *Kate Crackernuts.*
Rushdie, Salman. *The Ground beneath her Feet.*
Long, Asphodel. *In a Chariot Drawn by Lions: the search for the female in deity.*
Grey, Mary. *The Wisdom of Fools.*
Armitage, Simon. *Sir Gawain and the Green Knight.*
Starhawk. *The Spiral Dance.*
Fiorenza, Elizabeth Schussler. *But SHE Said.*
Fiorenza, Elizabeth Schussler. *Bread, Not Stone.*
Greenhalgh, Zohra. *Contrarywise.*
Byatt, A. S. *Angels and Insects.*
Heschel, Susannah. *On Being a Jewish Feminist.*
Bristowe, W. S. *The World of Spiders.*

Opie, Iona and Peter. *The Oxford Dictionary of Nursery Rhymes.*
Child, Francis James. *The English and Scottish Popular Ballads.*
Jones, Diana Wynne. *The Eight Days of Luke.*
Jones, Diana Wynne. *Fire and Hemlock.*
Basford, Kathleen. *The Green Man.*
Anderson, William. *Green Man.*
Judge, Roy. *Jack-in-the-Green.*
Graves, Robert. *The White Goddess.*
Williamson, Robin. *The Wise and Foolish Tongue.* (Also published under the title *The Craneskin Bag.*)
Kushner, Ellen. *Thomas the Rhymer.*
Barber, Antonia and Lynch, P. J. *Catkin.*
Briggs, Katherine. *An Encyclopedia of Fairies.*
Nancy Springer. *Fair Peril.*
Terry Pratchett. *Lords and Ladies.*

DANIEL COHEN

ACKNOWLEDGEMENTS

Francesca de Grandis encouraged me to write. Her editorial work on the stories was invaluable.

Judith Hampson and Miriam Scott gave additional editorial help on the stories.

Carol Christ gave me much support in writing.

Hugh Lupton and Eric Maddern, master storytellers, held annual storytelling retreats. These helped me find my voice as a storyteller, and provided the seeds for several of my stories.

Tony Long gave me information about tickling trout and snaring hares.

Asphodel Long, who is no longer with us, provided much encouragement and inspiration, and suggested themes for several stories.

Jan Henning was my co-editor on *Wood and Water* magazine for over twenty years, until it ceased publication; we greatly enjoyed producing it. Her understanding of the Folk is profound, and our discussions of Them, and of ballads and stories in general, have enriched my life. I wish she would write for a wider audience.

I am grateful to Professor James McCool, of the Mathematics Department of the University of Toronto, for allowing me to use his name in an incident that should have happened but did not.

In journeying to the places from which I tell these stories I have learned from many women, both those I know as friends and those I know only through their writings. There are also men with whom I have shared visions. My thanks and love to the Goddess who has shown herself to me through these women and men.

~~~~~~~~~

I am extremely grateful to Rabbi Lynn Gottlieb who allowed me to put words of hers (from the essay *The Secret* Jew in the book *On Being a Jewish Feminist*, edited by Susanna Heschel) into the mouth of the Interpreter in my story of that name.

I also thank the following for permission to quote from their works.

Rabbi Malka Drucker for a quote from an article entitled *Burn, Sisters, Burn* in the July 1st, 2003, issue of the online magazine *Awakened Woman* to be found at www.awakenedwoman.com.

Thomas Moore for a quote from *Care of the Soul*.

Alicia Ostriker for a quote from *Feminist Revision and the Bible*.

Martin Graebe for his song *Jack-in-the-Green*.

Betsy Rose for a quote from her song *Taste and See* on her cassette *In My Two Hands*.

Laurell Hamilton for a quote from *A Stroke of Midnight*.

David Higham Associates for a quote from Russell Hoban's *Riddley Walker*.

Equinox Publishing for permission to reprint my story *Taste and See*, which first appeared in *Patriarchs, Prophets and Other Villains*, edited by Lisa Isherwood (copyright Equinox Publishing 2007).

~~~~~~~~~

Articles and book reviews by Daniel Cohen, mainly on Goddess-related themes, can be found on his Web site http://www.decohen.com

ILLUSTRATIONS

Z*qhygoem created the sequence of fifteen stylistically related drawings. They are copyright © by him, and he may be contacted at z-qhygoem@talktalk.net for permission to reproduce them.

Wen Fyfe made the drawings for *The Heart of the Labyrinth*, *Face of Wisdom*, *Face of Dread*, *The Sleeping Beauty*, and the first drawing for *The Singer's Lost Love*. Cathy Dagg illustrated *Circe's Bard*.

The illustrations for *Maiden and Monster* and *The First Casualty of War* were taken from Greek vase decorations.

The photo of Minerva (Athene) is a greyscale version of a colour photo of a bas-relief from Herculaneum, taken by Ken Thomas and placed in the public domain by him. His original is online at http://commons.wikimedia.org/wiki/File:ADIPompeii-27527-3.jpg

The illustration for *Taste and See*, which I found online at http://commons.wikimedia.org/wiki/File:Figures_Adam_and_Eve_were_both_naked_%26_were_not_ashamed.jpg is from an eighteenth century volume of illustration to the Bible.

The second illustration to *What Wome Most Desire* is from Howard Pyle's *The Story of King Arthur and his Knights*, published in 1903.

The illustration to *The Biggest Dungheap in the World* is a greyscale version of a colour photo of a Roman statue of Heracles Resting in the Hermitage Museum, Saint Petersburg. The original photo is online at http://www.flickr.com/photos/25622716@N02/3055450836 and was taken by Andrew Bossi.. It is copyright by him but licensed by him under the Creative Commons Attribution Share-Alike 2.0 Generic License; the same license therefore applies to the version used here.

The second illustration to *The Interpreter* is a greyscale version of a colour photo of a keystone at Great Malvern Post Office. The original photo is online at http://www.geograph.org.uk/photo/1579271 and was taken by Bob Embleton. It is copyright by him but licensed by him under the Creative Commons Attribution Share-Alike 2.0 Generic License; the same license therefore applies to the version used here.

The other photographs in the text are of various items in the author's apartment, taken by him and copyright © by him.

The photograph of the author on the back page is by Peter Greenhalgh, but is copyrigh © by the author.

The front cover was designed by Marjorie Sutler.